The Complete Book of

GUN
COLLECTING

Other Gun Books by CHARLES EDWARD CHAPEL

THE ART OF SHOOTING

THE BOY'S BOOK OF RIFLES

FIELD, SKEET, AND TRAP SHOOTING

FORENSIC BALLISTICS (out of print)

GUN CARE AND REPAIR—A MANUAL OF GUNSMITHING

THE GUN COLLECTOR'S HANDBOOK OF VALUES

GUNS OF THE OLD WEST

SIMPLIFIED PISTOL AND REVOLVER SHOOTING

SIMPLIFIED RIFLE SHOOTING

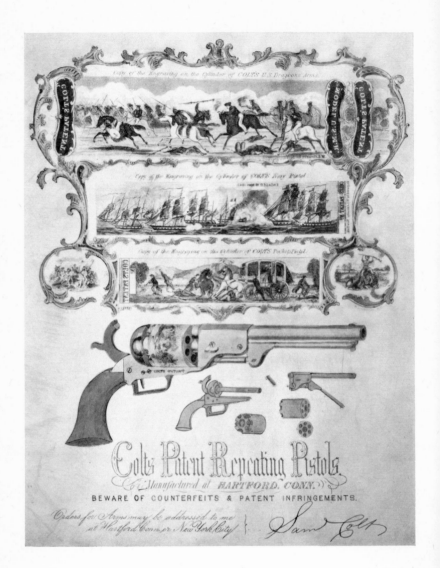

The Complete Book of

GUN
COLLECTING

By CHARLES EDWARD CHAPEL

First Lieutenant, United States Marine Corps (Retired)

ILLUSTRATED

COWARD-McCANN, INC.

NEW YORK

MANUFACTURED IN THE UNITED STATES OF AMERICA

VAN REES PRESS, NEW YORK

TO THE MEMORY OF MY GRANDFATHER, THE LATE

CHARLES HENRY JOHNSON,

A SERGEANT OF COMPANY D, 4TH WISCONSIN CAVALRY, UNION ARMY, THIS BOOK IS RESPECTFULLY DEDICATED IN THE HOPE THAT THOSE WHO COLLECT GUNS WILL NOT FORGET THE BRAVE MEN, LIVING AND DEAD, WHO HAVE CARRIED GUNS IN ORDER THAT WE MAY ENJOY LIBERTY AND A REPUBLICAN FORM OF GOVERNMENT IN THIS UNITED STATES

ACKNOWLEDGMENTS

The author thanks Mr. W. G. C. Kimball of Woburn, Massachusetts, for the photographs shown in Plates 2, 3, and 6; and thanks Mr. Harry L. Lindquist, of New York City, for the electrotypes of those photographs. The late Mr. George Smoots, of San Francisco, supplied the remaining plates which show arms from two great private collections.

The author also thanks the following gentlemen who devoted long hours of their valuable time to research, correspondence, and proofreading, in order that this book might be both accurate and interesting:

Mr. Robert Abels, New York City; Mr. Ed Agramonte, Yonkers, N.Y.; Mr. Langdon Albright, Jr., Portageville, N.Y.; Mr. Donald Bady, Forest Hills, N.Y.; Mr. De Witt Bailey, Storrs, Connecticut; Mr. Alexander V. Bartimo, Aledo, Illinois; Mr. Miller Bedford, New London, Conn.; Mr. Shelley Braverman, Athens, N.Y.; Mr. Robert Brownell, Montezuma, Iowa; Mr. Harold W. Cleveland, Redlands, California; Mr. Samuel E. Dyke, Allentown, Penna.; Mr. William B. Edwards, Skokie, Illinois; Mr. Robert Ellithorpe, Encino, California; Mr. Robert A. Erlandson, Baltimore, Maryland; Mr. Norm Flayderman, Greenwich, Conn.; Mr. Charles W. Fritz, Norwood, Ohio; Mr. J. Garnand Hamilton, Massilon, Ohio; Mr. George E. Hancock, Fairmount, Illinois; Mr. Gil Hebard, Knoxville, Illinois; Mr. Robert Held, New York City; Mr. Calvin Hetrick, New

7

Enterprise, Penna.; Mr. Marvin E. Hoffman, Miami Beach, Florida; Mr. Ed Howe, Cooper Mills, Maine; Major R. T. Huntington, Fort Lewis, Washington; Mr. George N. Hyatt, Wilmington, Delaware; Mr. Leon C. Jackson, Dallas, Texas; Mr. W. G. C. Kimball, Woburn, Mass.; Mr. Joe Kindig, Jr., York, Penna.; Mr. Wesley Kindig, Lodi, Ohio; Mr. G. Robert Lawrence, Santa Ana, California; Mr. Gilbert J. Levy, Hialeah, Florida; Colonel B. R. Lewis, Philadelphia, Penna.; Mr. Charles W. Moore, Schenevus, N.Y.; Mr. Milton F. Perry, Independence, Missouri; Mr. H. L. Remmel, Fayetteville, Arkansas; Mr. Ray Riling, Philadelphia, Penna.; Mr. Russell S. Goldstein, Fall River, Mass.; Mr. James E. Serven, Santa Ana, California; Mr. John W. Smith, Runnemede, N.J.; Mr. Samuel E. Smith, Markesan, Wisconsin; Mr. Henry M. Stewart, Wynnewood, Penna.; Mr. Peter H. Tillou, Buffalo, N.Y.; Mr. M. R. Waddell, Houston, Texas; Mr. Donald B. Webster, Jr., Kingston, Rhode Island; Mr. Frank Wheeler, Osborne, Kansas; Mr. Wes White, Freeville, N.Y.; Mr. Lewis Winant, Island Heights, N.J.; and Mr. Eldon G. Wolff, Milwaukee, Wisconsin.

CONTENTS

ILLUSTRATIONS

The Complete Book of

GUN
COLLECTING

I

STARTING
A GUN COLLECTION

*"I, and the gun, with our Brother Ball,
In whatever fight, we equal all."*

THIS JINGLE, FOUND CARVED ON A POWDER HORN OF THE Revolutionary War, partially explains why men of America and England love to collect old guns. The wood and iron in a firearm may be worth only a few cents, but behind the gun there is a story of danger, adventure, and high romance. To Americans the gun is a symbol of the battles we fought to make and preserve our national existence; to the English it is a reminder of their long struggle against royal tyrants and feudal barons. Even the civilization we boast about today can survive only when it is supported by the force of arms.

Most of us own at least one old gun that is the nucleus of an interesting and valuable collection. It may be a flintlock from the Revolution, a "cap-and-ball" from the Civil War, a Krag from the Spanish-American War, or a Springfield brought back from World War I. It may be merely an old shotgun which is still used to bring down a goose on the first day of the hunting season. Any one of these guns can arouse our interest in collecting; and whether we collect for the patriotic associations connected with guns, the mechanical progress they exhibit, or simply for the pure fun of the hobby, the result is the same—the love of guns is in our blood, and a number of questions about each gun come to mind. What is it? Who invented it? Who made it? Where was it made? Why was it designed differently from the other guns? Was it carried in a war? Is it rare today? What is it worth?

To answer these questions, and many more that are asked by the beginner in the gun-collecting hobby, this book was written. More than forty years ago the author started collecting guns, just as you may do, with an old war relic given him by a relative. There were books—dozens of them—on the use of guns in hunting, their mechanical details, and their historic evolution, but until the publication of the first edition of this book in 1939, not one book had ever been published to guide the beginner in choosing guns for a collection. Even magazines with gun departments neglected the novice and concentrated on expensive weapons beyond the reach of the beginner.

In these pages we shall show you how to collect for both fun and profit by explaining the hitherto undiscussed fundamental principles of appraising values, arranging an exhibit, and identifying desirable pieces. You will be taken along the highway of firearm progress, step by step, starting with the earliest gun, the hand cannon, and advancing through the successive periods of matchlock, wheel lock, flintlock, and cap-and-ball to the modern cartridge era. When you have learned to recognize these important types, we shall then examine the freaks and oddities of the gun world, and discuss the answers to such questions as these—What kinds of guns shall I collect? How can I recognize a valuable piece? Why is it that some old and rare guns are worth only a few dollars while others that are more common and not so old bring hundreds of dollars at a sale? Does a gun's condition affect its value? What should I do to take care of my guns? What is the best way to photograph a gun? Is there any profit to be made from buying and selling guns for collectors?

Actually to start building a gun collection, look in old attics and barns, visit the junk shops and secondhand dealers, tell your friends and relatives you are a gun collector, and write to all the gun dealers for their price lists and catalogues. You need not have any great amount of money to acquire valuable pieces. Many firearms will be given you, free, by people who are glad to get rid of their excess belongings, and you can often purchase extremely rare and desirable specimens for a few dollars. Rudolph J. Nunnemacher, for example, bought one of the extremely rare Ferguson breech-loading, flintlock rifles in an obscure junk shop at a price which represented little more than its value as scrap iron, and this piece is today one of the most outstanding exhibits of the Milwaukee Public Museum.

You will want to obtain the dealers' catalogues and price lists, not only to order guns you cannot acquire locally, but also for the more important reason that you can receive from their literature a wealth of information regarding the current trends in collecting, and the prevailing market prices for all types and conditions of guns. Most of the dealers illustrate their catalogues, but the majority of them describe their offerings in technical terms understandable only to the more advanced collectors. We have tried to explain these terms in simple language throughout this book; but if you are puzzled by such expressions as "sear" or "frizzen," in a catalogue, turn to the Glossary at the end of the text, and you will find the jargon of gun collectors translated into plain English.

The mention of dealers may conjure up ideas of prices beyond the budget of the beginner; it is quite true that they emphasize the more valuable pieces, just as any merchant will do, but it is surprising to find that more than fifty per cent of the items suitable for a representative collection can be bought for thirty dollars or less. Many of these lower-priced items are rarities, too; for the strange thing about the gun hobby is that values depend primarily upon popular demand, and only secondarily on age, rarity, or condition.

A good example of this situation is found in the case of flintlock pistols. One of the big dealers in antique arms obtained a number of Belgian flintlock pistols which were more than a century old. These were all in good working condition, complete with flints, brass-mounted, with 9-inch barrels and an over-all length of 15 inches. A person might think that the combination of good condition and extreme age would bring a high price, especially in view of the fact that most of the original flintlocks were converted to cap-and-ball weapons about 1845; but in spite of all these factors, the dealer sold the pistols for seven dollars apiece in 1936.

In 1936 a flintlock pistol, in the same condition, and of the same age, but made in the United States, was seldom sold by a dealer for less than twenty or thirty dollars. The difference in price is principally caused by the greater demand for American-made weapons in the United States. In starting your collection, you can obtain attractive pieces very reasonably if you select those which are less popular with the more experienced collectors. Then, when you decide to specialize in the more costly arms, you can sell or trade these early purchases to others, probably at a profit, for guns are a safer investment than stocks or bonds.

"Beginner's Luck" seems to exist in gun collecting just as it does in hunting and fishing. A few years ago we showed a Paterson Colt revolver to a friend who was just beginning to collect firearms, and we emphasized the desirability of examining the early Colts for the manufacturer's marks as a quick means of identification. The next day he returned, unwrapped a package, and grinned as he proudly displayed a revolver with that wording that always quickens a collector's pulse: "Patent Arms M'g. Co., Paterson, N.J. Colt's Pt." We knew that he was a poor man, and wondered how he could afford to buy a weapon then worth six or seven hundred dollars. When he explained that he had seen it in the window of a pawnshop and bought it for a few dollars, we decided that it was always worth while to tell beginners about the valuable guns as well as the common specimens, for they are often the ones who have the luck. That same revolver is today worth between $1,800 and $2,100, depending upon condition.

Value, in terms of dollars and cents, is important; but if you are a real collector—a man who loves guns for what they are and what they have been—the true value of guns is not monetary: instead it lies in their magic property of permitting you to escape from the humdrum world of reality and soar away into the realms of fancy where the Continental troops carry their flintlocks in review past George Washington; where Kentucky Riflemen under Andrew Jackson drive back the flower of the British Army at New Orleans; and where Berdan's Sharpshooter Regiment helps to save the Union in the Valley of the Potomac. In imagination you can follow Teddy Roosevelt to Cuba with his Roughriders, and sail with the Marines "from the Halls of Montezuma to the Shores of Tripoli." Know your guns, but do not forget the story behind the guns. There lies their true value!

II

ANCIENT GUNS

Hand Cannon, Matchlock,
and Arquebus

IF YOU WANT A COLLECTION WHICH ILLUSTRATES THE
progress of firearms from the primitive times to the present,
you will start with the weapon known as the hand cannon.
In its earliest form this was a simple metal tube, with a
bore varying from one-half inch to one inch in diameter,
fastened to a straight stick by wire, iron hoops, or leather.
It was loaded from the muzzle, and lighted there, too, until
some genius thought of having a "touch-hole" on the top,
near the breech. When loaded, a small amount of powder
was placed over the touchhole and a torch or a red-hot
iron was applied to ignite the charge.

Historians argue as to whether the hand cannon was
merely a miniature cannon or an independent design. They
also disagree regarding the date of the invention of the
cannon. Neither of these questions is important to the collector. It is sufficient to know that the earliest known examples of this type of gun definitely date from the fourteenth
century.

The straight stick gave way to stocks copied from the
crossbows, and these stocks were rested on top of the right
shoulder in firing, some of them having notches cut near

21

the butt to fit over the shoulder. To steady the aim and avoid some of the recoil, the foot soldier of that day had a forked stick which he jabbed into the ground and used as a rest, while his brother in the cavalry suspended the gun from his neck with a looped cord.

To aim the hand cannon, the gunner glanced over his right thumb as it lay on top of the stock, and this, like the shape and manner of holding the stock, was a holdover from the method used to aim the crossbow. Progress in the design of arms has always been slow; it was not until the beginning of the sixteenth century that the butt was enlarged and made to fit against the shoulder instead of resting on top.

It might be inferred that hand cannon were one-man affairs, but this was seldom the case. The gunpowder was weak and had to be loaded in quantity to give the bullet velocity enough to pierce the armor of the mounted knights. Even then the principal value of the guns lay in the noise of their explosions, the flashes, and clouds of smoke which terrified enemy soldiers who regarded firearms as the work of the devil. Tapestries portraying the battles of the sixteenth century show large hand cannon, carried and fired by two men, one man steadying the gun while the other aimed and lighted the charge. These were the "roaring culverins" mentioned by Macaulay; from ancient documents we know that they weighed from fifteen to twenty pounds apiece.

Hand cannon were first made of iron bars welded and strengthened by hoops and covered with leather; later, they were cast in bronze and iron. For ammunition, stones were the earliest missiles, followed by lead, brass, and iron balls.

The primitive gunpowder, called "serpentine powder," was a coarse meal; but in the fifteenth century the process of "corning" or forming the powder into grains was discovered. By varying the size of the grains, the strength, and hence the quantity, of powder used could be controlled; this led to the making of the one-man hand cannon typical of the latter part of the fifteenth century.

What happened to these early guns? Some were converted into matchlocks, the guns of the next ignition period; some were melted to provide metal for newer types of firearms; and still others rusted or corroded until they lost all semblance of guns. The beauty of modern weapons lies in the fact that their shape is adapted entirely to their purpose, but in ancient times guns were prized for their artistry as well as for their usefulness. Only about sixteen genuine European hand cannon are known to exist today.

Hand cannon within the reach of the collector of moderate means are mostly oriental pieces: Japanese and Chinese specimens that are seldom over one hundred years old. This is hard to believe; but the explanation is that the orientals were making hand cannon as late as 1800 because they were simple and cheap to cast, and served their purpose in the absence of anything better.

Hand cannon should not be confused with *lantakas*. A lantaka is a Malay cannon, made of brass or bronze, from twenty inches to seven feet in length, and usually provided with a swivel and pin for mounting on a boat. Very small ones, resembling hand cannon, are often offered collectors in lieu of the hand cannon, but these small lantakas are not weapons in the true sense; instead, they are saluting pieces, made small to economize on powder. They are often decorated with Chinese, Spanish, Portuguese, and Dutch words and symbols. Those marked with Arabic writing were carried by the Mohammedan tribes. A lantaka is an interesting addition to any collection, but it has no proper place in an exhibit of ancient guns.

The matchlock followed the hand cannon as an ignition type. It was developed about 1450, in Europe, and was manufactured in China and Japan as late as 1875. As an improvement on the hand cannon, it substituted a burning wick for the hot irons and torches used to light the priming powder in the older type; and this burning wick, called a "match," was carried to the touchhole by means of a piece of metal pivoted on the side of the barrel.

At first this metal was C-shaped, with the lower end of the "C" attached to the gun, the upper end being split open to hold the glowing end of the match. The shooter had no trigger; when he wanted to fire, he reached over with his right thumb and pushed the match against the touchhole.

The metal was next changed from a C-shape, to an S-shape, and became known as the "Serpentine." It was pivoted in the center of the "S," with the upper end holding the burning match and the lower part serving as a trigger. With this device, the soldier was able to aim and fire at the same time.

In the meantime, gunmakers moved the touchhole from the top to the side of the barrel, where they placed a little pan, called the "flash-pan," which held the priming powder for setting off the main charge. To the pan they added a vertical shield, called a "fence"; this prevented the blast of the explosion from blowing ashes back into the face of the shooter.

Various substances were tried in an effort to obtain a wick that would burn steadily, the final choice being salt-peter. The wick was soaked in a solution, dried, and then issued to the soldier in lengths of four or five feet. One end was attached to the serpentine, which was finally designed to hold the wick in a tube instead of a clamp; and the rest of the match was wrapped around the stock of the gun or left hanging. When the trigger was pulled, it had not only to bring the lighted end to the touchhole but also lift part of the weight of the slack portion of the match.

As the glowing match continued to grow shorter, the shooter had to keep shoving it through the tube, being sure that it projected far enough to light the priming powder, but not so far as to fall loosely to one side and thus miss the pan when the trigger was pulled. At the same time, he had to keep knocking the ashes off the end of the match or they would fall into the pan and weaken the force of the powder. These were all serious problems of the first, or "nonsnapping," type of matchlock. In an effort to overcome these difficulties, the second, or "snapping," type was developed late in the fifteenth or early in the sixteenth century.

The snapping matchlock was equipped with a spring and lever mechanism so that the serpentine, called the "cock," after about 1625, was held back by the spring until released by pulling the trigger, when the cock fell with a quick blow that not only lighted the priming powder in the pan but also knocked the ashes from the glowing end of the match with the force of the fall. The long match of the nonsnapping type was replaced by a short piece of match held in the cock by a tube instead of the former clamp. In its action, the snapping matchlock mechanism closely resembles the contemporary crossbow trigger-release device; so we cannot describe it as an advance in design so much as a clever adaptation of an ancient pattern.

Curiously enough, the snapping matchlock was made so that the cock fell toward the shooter instead of away from him as was the case with the nonsnapping type. This is true of earlier European guns, but oriental snapping matchlocks are almost always found with the cock falling away from the shooter.

All these details are important to the collector, for they enable him to assign a gun to its correct period and to be on his guard against mistakes. Like hand cannon, the matchlocks of European manufacture are rare and generally costly because only the carefully made and beautifully ornamented European matchlocks have survived the passing of the centuries. Oriental specimens, when genuine, cannot be described as common, but they are usually of such comparatively recent manufacture that it is possible to buy pieces in good condition at prices within the reach of the average individual.

The matchlock was followed by the wheel lock; but before we examine the next step in the progress of ignition methods we should explain the use of the word "Arquebus," also called "Harquebus." One dictionary defines it as "An obsolete portable firearm, at first having a matchlock operated by a trigger." The definition is good enough to serve the purpose of a crossword puzzle addict, but it is of little help to a gun collector. If you go further in your dictionary study, you will find that the word came into the English language from the French, where it was in turn derived from a Dutch or German word meaning a "gun with a hook." There lies the clue to the gun collector's riddle.

Arms historians have argued for centuries about which guns to class as arquebuses. One of the earliest references to the use of a gun of this name is found in the Swiss records of their capture of Neuregensberg in 1386. Contemporary pictures show that the Swiss were using matchlocks with butts which dropped below the barrel line, as distinguished from the earlier matchlocks and the hand cannon designed with the straight stock copied from crossbows. It is believed that this drop in the stock was the "hook" which gave the arquebus its name, the purpose being to reduce the recoil from the heavy powder charge that was transmitted undiminished to the shoulder of the shooter in guns with a straight stock.

Our explanation seems to be the popular one in America, but European collectors have three other theories about the arquebus. First, some of them say that the "hook" referred to the serpentine, or cock, found in the ignition mechanism of the matchlock. Second, others say that there was an actual hook, made of metal, and that its purpose was to steady the aim and reduce the recoil when the soldier was firing over a wall. Third, still others believe that there was a metal hook, but that it was used to attach the gun to the soldier's belt when not being fired.

The late George Cameron Stone, an outstanding authority on arms and armor, who bequeathed many of his most valuable pieces to the Metropolitan Museum of Art in New York, disregarded the arguments of the collectors and summed up the whole situation correctly in his book,

*A Glossary of the Construction, Decoration, and Use of
Arms and Armor,* when he said:

"ARQUEBUS, HARQUEBUS. Originally a heavy
matchlock gun; later the name was applied to wheel-lock
guns, and finally came to mean a gun of fine workmanship
as distinguished from the musquet, or common military
arm."

The importance of this rather lengthy discussion of the
arquebus lies in the fact that in collecting guns you will
find "arquebus" or "harquebus" used over and over again
by dealers, museum curators, and brother collectors, to
describe both matchlocks and wheel locks of every possible
size, shape, and description. Require them to give full details of description and you will know what they are talking
about. By itself, the word is so general in coverage that it
is almost worthless in the vocabulary of the collector.

How effective were these ancient guns? Montaigne, writing in 1585, said that the actual effect was small, but German and Swiss hunters of that era, presumably using rifled
arms, were killing deer and bears at ranges up to 250 yards.

A contrary view was expressed by an Italian writer who
reported his observations in 1430, more than a century and
a half before Montaigne. Describing the siege of Lucca, he
said:

"The Luccanians invented a new weapon. In their hands,
they held a block of wood about one and one-half yards
long, fastened to which was an iron tube filled with sulfur
and saltpeter which threw iron bullets by the force of fire.
The blow, when it struck, brought certain death, and neither
armor nor shield were a sufficient protection; then, not seldom did a single bullet penetrate a file of two or three men."

It was this ability of the common man, armed with a gun, to kill knights in armor that later led to the decline of knighthood and the rise of the foot soldier as the chief reliance of the king. As the peasants learned their importance in the military affairs of the rulers, they gradually threw off their yokes and demanded more and more rights until they eventually reached a fair degree of freedom.

Some arms historians believe that the crossbow led to the decline of armored knights and the importance of the foot soldier. Most arms historians take the position that gun-armed foot soldiers led to the gradual elimination of armored knights and some small increase in the importance of peasants. The broad view is that no throwing-off of the yokes of tyranny can be attributed to firearms any more than to other weapons in the world's history.

Thus we find that the gun is not all wood and iron; back of it is a story, a story of men who depended on firearms to find happiness for themselves and their descendants. In the next chapter, we shall continue the progress of ignition with an examination of the wheel lock, the gun that made possible the use of firearms in hunting and home defense.

MATCHLOCK AND WHEEL LOCK PISTOLS

Early Guns—Top to Bottom: M-2, Japanese Matchlock Pistol; M-3, Japanese Matchlock Pistol; M-4, Japanese Matchlock Pistol; M-15, Japanese Percussion Pistol; M-10, Italian Wheel Lock Cavalry Pistol, Circa 1640; M-11, Italian Wheel Lock Cavalry Pistol, Circa 1640, Caliber .51, 14″ smoothbore octagon barrel, 21½″ over-all; M-5, Japanese Matchlock Pistol; M-7, Japanese Matchlock Pistol; M-9, Japanese Matchlock Pistol; M-6, Japanese Matchlock Pistol; M-3289, Japanese Matchlock Pistol; M-8, Japanese Matchlock Pistol.

The tube-type serpentine matchlocks are not regarded by some experts as a later development. They were designed to hold a small piece of unlit tinder which was set aglow from the match, prior to shooting. This is an alternate form, sometimes called a "tinder lock" and is found on most Japanese matchlocks which were not designed to carry the long match cord but only a piece of unlit tinder. Shooters, both European and Japanese, lit the tinder in this type from the burning match cord.

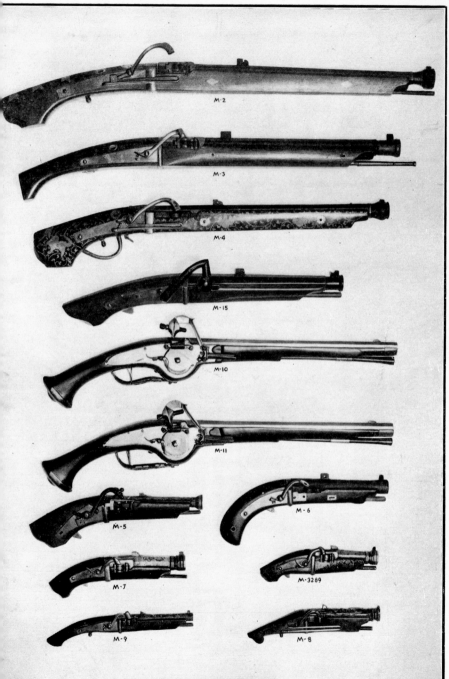

M-2

M-3

M-4

M-15

M-10

M-11

M-5

M-6

M-7

M-3289

M-9

M-8

PLATE NO. 1

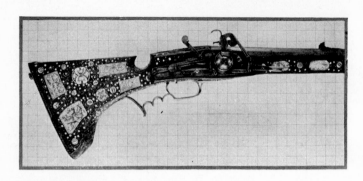

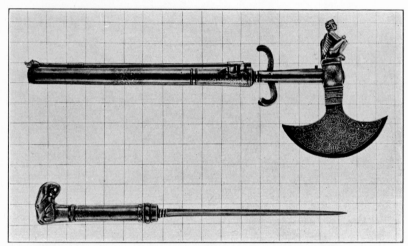

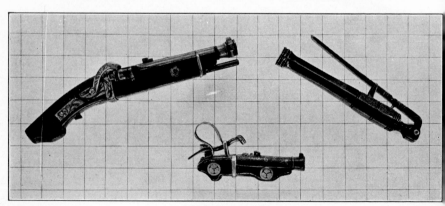

PLATE No. 2

MATCHLOCK, WHEEL LOCK, AND
HAND CANNON

The Guns Were Photographed Against a Background of One-Inch Grid Lines to Indicate Size.

Courtesy W. G. C. Kimball

Combined Matchlock and Wheel Lock

Combination Matchlock Pistol, Ax and Dagger, India. The collection of combination arms is a specialty in itself. The inclusion of the matchlock in the combination, the artistic workmanship, and the excellent condition of this weapon make it extremely valuable.

Left to right: Matchlock Pistol, bronze Hand Cannon and Hand Cannon. The two hand cannons are both conversions. One is a serpentine and the other a detonator, both of which were added subsequent to the true hand cannon period, but not in Japan. The matchlock came in with the gun from Europe, avoiding the series of developments which the gun went through in Europe. A detonator depends upon a crushing of the "percussion" material, instead of striking a true blow. The two arms in this lower picture at the left and bottom are definitely Japanese and the third is probably Japanese.

III

WHEEL LOCK, PYRITES LOCK, SNAPHANCE, AND MIQUELET

———————

THE WHEEL LOCK, INVENTED BY LEONARDO DA VINCI about 1480, was first made in Italy, and first commercially successful in Germany about 1515. In its lock a piece of pyrites is held in the jaws of a cock, called a "dog leg," and pressed against a rough-edged wheel that comes up through the bottom of the pan holding the priming powder. The wheel is connected to a "V" spring compressed with a keylike object called the "spanner." When the trigger is pulled, the tension on the spring is released, and the wheel revolves against the pyrites, thus making the sparks which ignite the priming powder, which in turn sets off the main charge in the barrel through a touchhole. This is similar in action to a modern cigarette lighter.

The principle back of the wheel lock is nothing more than the old flint-and-steel method of starting a fire; but the mechanism required to apply this to gun ignition was so complicated and difficult to make that principally kings and noblemen could afford to own a wheel lock, with the result that most privately owned guns through the whole wheel-lock period were of the older, matchlock type. Furthermore, in the early days of the wheel lock, conservative people had their guns made with two locks, one match and one wheel, to insure themselves against the failure of either lock to function. Later, in the flintlock era, we find both flint and wheel locks on the same gun.

Collectors recognize several distinct types of locks. The wheel may be either inside or outside of the lock plate. It may be exposed or covered with a guard to prevent the sharp edges of the wheel from tearing the clothes of the shooter. Instead of having the spring work directly on the wheel, there is a chain from the spring to the wheel, something like the chain on a bicycle. There may be one barrel and two locks, or there may be several barrels, each with its own lock. Probably the oddest design of all has one barrel arranged so that two charges can be loaded in the barrel, one on top of the other; the front load is fired first, and then the one behind. Obviously, the latter pattern was dangerous if the shooter forgot what he was doing and fired the rear charge first, for then they both went off at once, ruined the gun, and crippled or killed the shooter.

The wheel lock, like each new ignition type, was developed to overcome the defects of the former type. The matchlock was simple and cheap to make, but it was hard to keep the match burning in damp weather and it was slow to prepare for firing. On the other hand, the wheel lock was complicated and expensive, but it was independent of weather conditions, it could be concealed on the person, it was more accurate when fired from horseback, there was no burning match to reveal the presence of the shooter to wild game or an enemy, and there was no delay in preparing to fire. These superiorities of the wheel lock made it the principal military and sporting weapon from the date of its invention to the middle of the seventeenth century.

In quality, the wheel lock varied from crude military guns to beautiful arms with deep engraving, tasteful carving, and inlays of gold, silver, mother-of-pearl, and ivory. On all of them the mechanism was hard to keep in working order; when anything went wrong, it required the services of a skilled locksmith to make repairs. When simpler and better gun types appeared, the wheel locks were junked unless they were regarded as masterpieces of art; and this explains why most of the specimens available today are valuable.

The demand for wheel locks in good condition is great, the supply is very limited. Through good times and bad, the price has been as steady as that of diamonds. The value depends upon the design, construction and decoration. In 1947, specimens in fine condition with elaborate ornamentation sold for at least five hundred dollars apiece, but in 1960 fine wheel locks sold for fifteen hundred dollars. However, a collector could occasionally buy one for as low as two or three hundred dollars in 1960, but this value was an exception to the general average.

Specialists in American martial arms often include English wheel locks, for they were used in colonial days by men of wealth and position; but the collector need not be surprised to find German or Italian names on the locks, since the English generally imported the ignition mechanism from the Continent. The historical background gives the English arms a special interest of their own, but the most beautiful specimens are generally Italian or German.

In an emergency, flint was used in wheel locks to make

the sparks, but it was so hard that it wore down the edge of the wheel, so iron pyrites, a brassy-yellow mineral commonly called "fool's gold," was placed in the cock for the wheel to rub against. Flint and steel, or pyrites and steel, had been used for centuries in starting fires, but it was long after the introduction of the wheel lock before gunmakers found a way to simplify the design of the locks.

Historically, the pyrites lock is discussed by advanced gun collectors as a traditional type somewhere between the wheel lock and the true flintlock, but its only resemblance to the wheel lock lies in the use of pyrites. It probably developed from the matchlock, which it closely copies in appearance and pattern with only two important exceptions. First, instead of a serpentine holding a match, the pyrites lock has a pair of jaws holding the pyrites, called the "cock." Second, an upright steel plate is provided for the pyrites to strike against. This plate was called at various times either the "frizzen" or the "battery," and it was eventually hinged to serve a secondary purpose as a cover to keep the rain and the wind out of the priming pan.

The typical pyrites lock can be recognized by the fact that the cock is at the end of an extremely long hammer arm which is set far back, near the end of the lock plate, the object being to provide a long, scraping contact, rather than a quick, sharp blow, against the steel. A bigger flow of sparks was produced and also there was less breakage of the pyrites.

Another distinguishing feature of the pyrites lock is the curve in the outline of the hammer which gives it part of the scraping effect against the steel; when the gun is fired, the cock lies almost parallel with the axis of the bore. Still another characteristic is the simplicity of the mechanism inside the lock. These details are given because there are few collectors or dealers who can recognize the distinctions between the pyrites lock and the later pre-flintlock types, with the result that they list a pyrites lock as a snaphance or flintlock, and excuse themselves by saying that the pyrites lock is so rare that it is seldom found outside of museums. Some arms historians refuse to recognize the pyrites lock as a distinct type and prefer to treat it as just one of many early snap-type devices.

Following the pyrites lock, came the snaphance, the immediate predecessor of the true flintlock. The word is of Dutch origin, and originally meant either "chicken thieves" or "pecking fowls," the first from the fact that robbers preferred this weapon to the matchlock that exposed them at night; and the second from the use of the words "cock" and "hen" in referring to the cock and the steel plate it struck. The derivation of the gun's name is more interesting than important, but the collector may avoid confusion if he notes that the snaphance has also been spelled "snaphaunce," and "snapharmce" in English.

A true snaphance has the battery (frizzen) and the pan cover made in separate pieces, as distinguished from the typical flintlock, which has the battery and pan cover in one piece, attached to the pan by a hinge, so that when the flint hits the steel battery the pan cover flies open and exposes the priming powder to the sparks. This separate pan cover of the snaphance was copied from the wheel lock. A rod engages when the gun is cocked and the pan cover stays closed. The pan cover snaps open when the trigger is pulled and the cock snaps. The pan cover opens forward to expose the priming powder.

The snaphance was first made about 1550, only thirty-five years after the wheel lock became commercially successful in Germany. As a distinct type, it began to disappear in some parts of the world with the coming of the fully developed flintlock. It remained the chief type of gun lock in Italy until about 1780 and in the Near East until about 1914. Early historians did not differentiate between the words "flintlock" and "snaphance." The idea of regarding them as separate types is comparatively modern and largely the work of arms collectors. Scottish snaphances are generally very valuable, but North African snaphance shoulder arms in 1960 could be bought for $100 or less, depending upon condition, and fine Brescian snaphance pistols in 1960 sometimes sold for about $350.

Like the snaphance, the Spanish lock called the "miquelet" derived its name from its inventors, the Spanish or Portuguese marauders known as *miquelites* or *miguelitos,* who adopted this arm for much the same reason that the Dutch or German robbers chose the snaphance. In spite of the Spanish origin of the name, it is a matter of record that Emperor Charles V sent to Germany for two gunsmiths, Simon and Pecho Macuarte, in 1530. Apparently their real names were Simon and Peter Markhardt and it is possible that the miquelet lock was invented in Germany. However, all guns known to have been made by these men are wheel locks. Incidentally, the oldest snaphance in Spain shows an oriental influence.

The miquelet lock has a heavy outside mainspring and cock, as distinguished from the snaphance lock with its mechanism inside the plate where it cannot be easily injured. In this, the miquelet is inferior to the Dutch gun; but the miquelet has the advantage of a hammer and pan cover in one piece, so that the pan is uncovered when the flint hits the frizzen. In contrast with the pyrites lock, the miquelet cock delivers a quick, powerful blow instead of a long scraping contact, and it uses flint.

Another feature of the miquelet is a safety catch, made necessary by a faulty design permitting the cock to slip when in the "half-cock" position. This safety catch consists of a bolt at right angles to the lock plate, and a nose on the front of the cock that rests on the bolt at the half-cock. The first part of the pull on the trigger releases the bolt and leaves the cock free to strike the frizzen. You can recognize the miquelet by this safety catch when the other characteristics are missing. The mechanism, for instance, was placed inside the lock plate in models used as late as 1850, but the safety catch varied little from the first to the last.

Guns with miquelet locks, military and sporting, short and long, were carried in the Balkans, Turkey, Egypt, and Persia long after flintlocks became obsolete, and they are still found in the hands of African tribes. The long period of time and the wide distribution for the miquelet prevented the destruction that made other early firearms scarce. Today, desirable specimens can be obtained sometimes for forty or fifty dollars, but the value varies with the quality of the workmanship, the fidelity to type, the amount of ornamentation, and the general condition. They are available in a great range of lengths and calibers and with the marks of gunsmiths of many nations. Any collector, whether he is rich or poor, can afford a good example of a miquelet.

In our next chapter we shall discuss the true flintlock type, the one for which the pyrites lock, the snaphance, and the miquelet paved the way.

Some historians insist that the development of the pyrites lock, the snaphance, and the miquelet was parallel and not consecutive. Whether this is true or not, it is agreed that they were the predecessors of the true flintlock type, which is so closely identified with early American history.

IV

FLINTLOCKS

—————〰〰〰—————

Ⓘ N ITS FINAL FORM, THE FLINTLOCK HAD A BATTERY OR frizzen (whichever term you prefer) which was made in one piece with the pan cover and was knocked out of the way to uncover the priming powder in the pan when the flint struck the steel. No one can give any definite date for the emergence of the flintlock as a definite ignition type, for this was not an invention but a result of slow development. However, we can say that the true flintlock probably dates from about 1625. With this arm, our ancestors fought under the English flag in the French and Indian Wars in Colonial days, and against the English in the Revolution and the War of 1812. Until about 1940 the flintlock was used in regions where percussion caps and cartridges were scarce but flint was plentiful. It was this natural supply of a spark-making material that kept the flintlock in the hands of hunters and soldiers until the percussion system of ignition came into general use between 1835 and 1845.

Collectors often ask how they can identify a Colonial flintlock. This is an extremely difficult question to answer, for many of the gunsmiths did not mark their guns with names or dates, and they usually imported the locks from Europe, since lockmaking was a special trade in itself. When a gun does have the name of the maker and he is known to have worked in America before the Revolution, it is fairly safe to say that the particular piece is really "Colonial." In the absence of such definite information, any attempt at identification is at best merely an intelligent guess.

The same difficulty arises when we attempt to say whether or not a firearm was "Revolutionary." In the Colonial period the Americans had been discouraged from manufacturing any finished products for themselves; instead, they were expected to furnish raw materials to Great Britain and receive in exchange the manufactured articles, even though these same objects could be made more economically in the Colonies. This may seem unfair from our present viewpoint, but it was in accordance with the traditional European policy of regarding colonies as cows to be milked by the mother country. The result was that the Colonists imported most of their guns of the better grade and bought abroad the locks which they installed on the guns they made here for hunting and home defense. Here and there some obscure gunsmith turned out weapons equal to most of those made in Europe, but the military arms were those furnished by England.

The traditional British shoulder weapon was the Brown Bess. This, together with the French Charleville Musket and the Swiss-German Rifle, provided the patterns for our American-made long arms of the Revolution, and influenced the design of the first arms we made after independence was secured. All three of these foreign guns were flintlock muzzle-loaders, but the British and French arms were smoothbores while the German weapon was rifled. In describing arms, the word "musket" usually implies an unrifled bore, but it is often loosely used to include any military shoulder weapon.

We have mentioned the foreign arms because they are intimately associated with the Revolution. In the spring of 1775, "Committees of Safety" were appointed in each of the thirteen colonies to arm the patriots for the coming struggle with England; and each Committee of Safety in turn chose gunsmiths to make weapons and appointed agents to gather guns already in existence which might be suitable for military use. The best of the three foreign guns was the Swiss-German Rifle. Gunsmiths in Pennsylvania had already modified the original design of the rifle so much that it had lost most of its original characteristics and could be reasonably described as a native weapon; but the Pennsylvania Rifle, commonly called the "Kentucky Rifle," could not be made quickly in quantities, so the various Committees relied principally on gunsmiths who contracted to supply smoothbores.

For a long time it was thought that the Committee of Safety muskets followed the patterns of the British Brown Bess and the French Charleville; but now, thanks to the painstaking research of L. D. Satterlee, of Detroit, Michigan, we think that many of the muskets made for the Committees followed the British Brown Bess type, and that the French musket was not widely copied until after the end of the Revolution. It is true that French locks are sometimes found on muskets definitely known to have been made for the Committees of Safety, but these muskets were also equipped with German, Austrian, Dutch, or any other locks which the gunsmiths happened to have on hand.

It has been estimated that there were between two and five hundred makers of arms in the Colonies at the time of the Revolution, and that at least two hundred made weapons for the Committees of Safety; so it is obvious that no set of specifications would cover any and all arms rightfully entitled to be called "Committee of Safety." Those we have examined ranged from .70 to .80 in caliber, the average being about .75, which is the approximate caliber of the average British Brown Bess used as a pattern for the gunsmiths.

Like the Brown Bess, the barrel of these Committee muskets was fixed to the stock by lugs under the barrel held by sliding pins through the stock. Some specimens have barrels averaging between 39 and 42 inches, with a total over-all length between 54½ and 57½ inches. Here again we run into a difficulty, for the popularity of the Pennsylvania-German (Kentucky) Rifle was beginning to influence the makers in favor of longer barrels, since there are some Committee Muskets with an over-all length of about 60 inches.

As we have seen, the agents of the Committees were sent out to pick up anything that would shoot. They scoured the country thoroughly and brought back such a miscellaneous collection of junk that Benjamin Franklin, whose judgment has seldom been questioned, seriously advocated arming the soldiers with bows and arrows!

Anyone, whether he was a gunsmith or not, who would sign a contract with a Committee and provide surety for performance of the contract, was set to work. The result was a chaotic condition of ammunition supply for the various calibers of guns on the part of Washington's officers, and a still greater confusion for the arms collectors of today.

Arms made between the spring of 1775 and the end of the Revolution in 1783 may be described as "Revolutionary," but to list them accurately as Committee of Safety Arms requires some sort of proof that they were made or obtained at the orders of one of the Committees. Experts are able to do this in only a few instances; the beginning collector must therefore rely on the honesty and judgment of others until the historians can give us more definite information about the guns of the Revolution.

The British Brown Bess Flintlock Musket, caliber about .75, was carried by the American Colonists in the French and Indian Wars, in the campaigns against the hostile redskins, and against the British themselves in the Revolution; for we must remember that our ancestors were, until the Declaration of Independence, loyal subjects of the Crown and thus entitled to draw the official British musket from the King's officers for use by the provincial militia.

To decide whether or not a particular specimen of Brown Bess was used during the Revolution or not is far from easy because there were few changes in construction details during the reigns of the four Georges, covering the period between 1714 and 1830, when the letters "G.R." standing for "George Rex," were marked on each Brown Bess musket. However, when the name of a gunsmith, or a date, is found on a musket, the work becomes less. Private manufacturers such as Sharpe, Edge, D. Egg, Grice, H. Nock, the Ketlands, and other English gunsmiths of the flintlock period, used their own private marks and the gunmakers' guilds had their marks.

"Tower" usually means the gun was inspected in the Tower of London, although it sometimes refers to the armory in Birmingham. "Dublin" or "D.C." (for Dublin Castle) is an inspection mark, although it was also used to mark arms surrendered to the English authorities in Dublin after Irish rebellions. An additional clue is the broad arrow; this signifies government ownership, and was first used for that purpose in the reign of King George I (1714-1727); it is still used today by the British.

If the barrel is stamped with a pair of crossed scepters, with the letters "BGP" placed in the angles formed by the crossing of the scepters, we know that the gun was not made until after the Revolution, for this mark was first used by the Birmingham proof house in 1813. Crossed scepters found on a gun without the letters are not inconsistent with a Revolutionary production, but it is apparent that the whole matter of fixing dates of manufacture and the use of guns in the flintlock period is a task that even experts prefer to avoid.

Gun historians for many years thought that the Brown Bess was originally named for Queen Elizabeth I (1558-1603) because she ordered one of her regiments equipped with matchlock guns with browned barrels and fittings, but now we believe that there is no justification for this legend. The name persisted in the popular fancy through the successive periods of the matchlock, wheel lock, and flintlock; it was not dropped until the British Army adopted the percussion system of ignition in 1836.

Next to the Brown Bess, the most widely copied foreign long arm was the German rifle, but few of its original features were retained and we have chosen to describe this weapon in detail in a chapter on the Kentucky Rifle.

The third foreign arm that greatly influenced our history was the French Model 1763 Flintlock Musket, caliber .69, commonly called the "Charleville Model" after the chief city of its manufacture. This was one of the first weapons imported by the Continental Congress, shipments being landed at Portsmouth, New Hampshire, and at Philadelphia, in 1777, supplemented by some that Lafayette brought with him the same year.

The Charleville was not only used in the Revolution but was copied closely in designing the U.S. Model 1795 Flintlock Musket, the first regulation United States shoulder arm made after the War. The Charleville used a caliber .69, one-ounce, lead ball, and that led the United States to choose this caliber for infantry muskets made at the Springfield Armory from its founding to the adoption of rifling in the place of smoothbores with the model of 1842 (1841).

The pistols of the Colonial and Revolutionary periods also follow in the same paths as the long arms, most of them being either European-made guns, or American-made weapons modeled after European patterns. The same general principles we apply in determining whether or not a musket is Revolutionary or Colonial are used in identifying pistols with these periods. If you have a firearm handed down in your family from ancestors who fought in Colonial wars or the war of the Revolution, your family tradition on the subject is valuable to you, and you should feel proud to possess such a historic weapon; but if you ever wish to dispose of it, do not be disappointed if an advanced collector or a dealer examines it carefully for identifying marks.

Representative specimens of regulation U.S. flintlock long arms are U.S. Models 1795, 1808, 1812, 1816, 1821, 1835, and 1841 (the latter also being called Model 1842). All of these are caliber .69 muzzleloaders and all are called muskets because they are smoothbores except the Model

1841 (1842) which is a rifle because it has a grooved bore.
The first six are known as muskets, since they are smoothbores, while the model of 1842 is called a rifle because the
bore is grooved.

The U.S. Model 1795 was not only the first official
United States musket but was also the first weapon made
by the U.S. Armory at Springfield, Massachusetts, established by Congress in 1794. You can identify it by the
"U.S." in script on the lock plate under a spread eagle between the cock and the pan. "SPRINGFIELD" is in a
curve behind the cock and across the lock plate. The barrel
is marked "U.S." with an eagle's head and the proof mark
"V.P." It is 60 inches long, the barrel is 44¾ inches long,
and the arm weighs 8⅞ pounds. These figures vary considerably with different specimens, largely because stand-
ardization was unknown then. It was made not only at
Springfield, but also by private contractors, such as Eli
Whitney, J. McCormick, E. Buell, and E. Brown; and it
was also made at the Harpers Ferry Armory.

To a beginner, all of the models we have listed look very
similar to one another. Even the experts argue as to whether
or not some of the models are distinct models or merely
variations of previous models. Some experts advise a beginner to first acquire U.S. Models 1795, 1812, 1816, and
1835, because these show distinct changes in design. Detailed descriptions of all U.S. martial arms are given in the
latest revised edition of the author's book, *The Gun Collector's Handbook of Values*.

Turning from the U.S. flintlock shoulder arms to the
regulation U.S. flintlock pistols, we find that there were
pistols purchased by the Committees of Safety, and by the

LOUIS XVI DUELING PISTOLS

Beautiful pair of Flintlock, Louis XVI, dueling pistols by LePage, of Versailles, France, who was the court armorer before Boutet. In this set, Boutet's name is engraved in the inside of the locks, while LePage signed his name on the outside. The pistols have gold and silver inlay, beautiful carving, and unusual beading around the handles, together with checkered wood and ivory-tipped rods. The great demand for the work of LePage and Boutet, the rarity of these pieces, and the fact they are in perfect condition make them a museum exhibit.

Photo by The Kimball Arms Co.

SAXON WHEEL LOCK DAG

This Saxon Wheel Lock Dag is dated 1591, and came from the Dresden Museum. Almost all of the gun is inlaid with ivory. It has a half octagon barrel, and is caliber .65. Its great age does not by itself determine value, but there is a great demand by collectors of European weapons for early wheel locks in fine condition.

Photo by The Kimball Arms Co.

SAXON PETRONEL

This Saxon Petronel from the famous Spitzer collection was made in the Milanese style of Azzamina, with beautifully inlaid hunting scenes on both sides of the full-length stock. Both lock and barrel are inlaid with gold and finely etched. There is a crucifix in ivory on the back of the stock, with a figure on each side. This is a wheel lock gun, the type that preceded the flintlock. The caliber is .58.

Photo by The Kimball Arms Co.

SAM BOONE KENTUCKY RIFLE

This is an extremely rare and historical Kentucky flintlock by Sam Boone, nephew of Daniel Boone, who moved to Pennsylvania and started gunmaking in 1768. The barrel bears his signature and carries the original browning. Total length is 57", with a 42" octagon barrel. The caliber is .42, with 7 deep grooves. It has a Ketland lock. The stock is of fine tiger flame maple, with elaborate carving on the left side; silver moon on the cheek piece; and a silver name plate on the back of the grip. The four pins that fasten the barrel to the stock go through into four silver half moons.

Photo by The Kimball Arms Co.

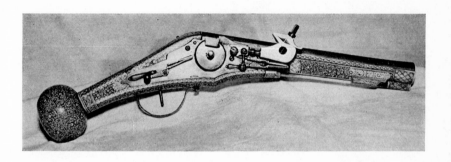

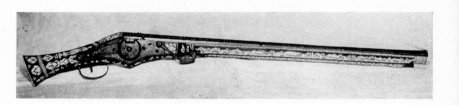

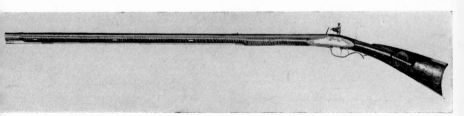

PLATE No. 3

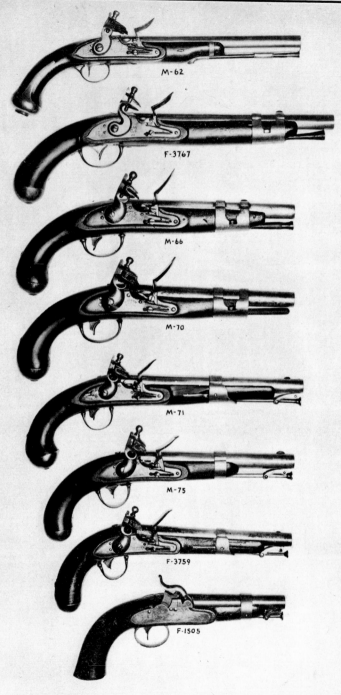

M-62

F-3767

M-66

M-70

M-71

M-75

F-3759

F-1505

PLATE NO. 4

UNITED STATES MARTIAL PISTOLS

M-62, Harpers Ferry, Flintlock Pistol, Model 1806
F-3767, U.S. Martial Pistol, Springfield Model 1818
M-66, S. North, Flintlock Pistol, Model 1816
M-70, S. North, Flintlock Pistol, Model 1813
M-71, S. North Flintlock Pistol, Model 1819
M-75, U.S. Johnson Flintlock Pistol, Model 1836
F-3759, J. J. Henry, U.S. Martial Pistol, Model 1827
F-1505, N. P. Ames Box-Lock Navy Pistol, Model 1843

Continental Congress, as we have already said, but the problem of accurate identification of these early pistols is too difficult for the beginner. However, *any American-made flintlock firearm is an interesting and comparatively valuable addition to any gun collection.* Most of the flintlocks were altered to percussion ignition; they are scarce in their original form, whether they were made for the United States forces, or for sale to individuals.

The earliest-known regulation U.S. flintlock pistol is the Model 1799-1800, North & Cheney, patterned after the French model of 1777, which it closely resembles, and made at Berlin, Connecticut, by Simeon North, and his brother-in-law, Elisha Cheney, a clockmaker who played little part in the manufacture or design of this pistol. It is caliber .69; the barrel is 8½ inches long, round, smoothbore; the total length is 14½ inches, and it weighs 3 pounds 4 ounces. The frame is brass; the only wood is in the grips on the handle. It is marked NORTH & CHENEY BERLIN or S. NORTH & E. CHENEY BERLIN. This is one of the great rarities in the firearms world. Two thousand were made and delivered to the government, but they have mostly disappeared "with the snows of yesteryear."

The U.S. Model 1806 Army and Navy Pistol, caliber .54, is 16½ inches long with a 10-inch barrel. Advanced collectors argue about the existence of rifling in this pistol when it was manufactured. Less than 5,000 were made, and like most of the other early pistols, this is a rarity. It is marked "Harpers Ferry," with the usual eagle, "U.S.," and the date of manufacture (1806, 1807, or 1808).

The U.S. Model 1808 Navy Pistol, caliber .69, smoothbore, is another one of Simeon North's pistols, being marked

"S. North, Berlin, Con., U. States," and the eagle. There is a belt hook on the left, and the butt has a shape approaching what collectors call the "birdshead." It is 16¼ inches long with a 10-inch round barrel.

Simeon North pistols are probably regarded more highly by flintlock collectors than any of the other government models; and they differentiate between them, not only by model dates and calibers, but also according to their place of manufacture, since he opened a larger plant in Middletown, Connecticut, in 1813, and put his son, Reuben, in charge of the old plant at Berlin, Connecticut. His Navy pistols are usually rated higher than his Army models, and his dueling pistols are not only rare but quite valuable. After the Model of 1808, the following were made:

U.S. Model 1811, caliber .69, smoothbore, same marks as the 1808.

U.S. Model 1813, caliber .69 with barrel band, marked "S. NORTH MIDLN. CON."

U.S. Model 1807 Pistol, caliber .69, marked "Springfield," "U.S.," with an eagle, and the *year of manufacture,* either 1815 or 1818 inclusive. These are not separate models, as a beginner might easily think. Some had an English-made lock with "Dale" stamped on the inside surface of the lock plate.

U.S. Model 1816, caliber .54, "S. North" "Midln. Con." marks.

S. North Pistol, Model 1817, caliber .54, but marked on lock like Model 1819.

U.S. Model 1819 Army and Navy, caliber .54, "S. North" and "Midltn. Con." marks; one specimen is known with "Middletown" spelled out in full, which is unusual, but this specimen had been converted to percussion fire.

U.S. Model 1826 Army and Navy, caliber .54, made and marked by S. North, J. J. Henry, and W. L. Evans, with dates of manufacture from 1827 to 1831, and possibly to 1835, for the J. J. Henry only.

U.S. Model 1836 Army Pistol, caliber .54; pattern models were made at Springfield, but usual specimens were made and marked by A. Waters, and R. J. Johnson. This model was made as late as 1844; it was the last of the U.S. flintlock pistols, and many were converted to percussion fire.

Flintlock arms to be fired from the hand were usually single-barrel weapons. Next in the frequency of manufacture were the guns with several barrels; these might have a lock for each barrel, or an arrangement whereby one lock fired the barrels in turn, with the barrels either sliding or revolving into position. Still rarer were the true revolvers, with a single barrel and a cylinder which revolved to present loads in the chambers of the cylinder in succession.

The revolving principle is as old as firearms, for it was first tried in the days of the hand cannon, but it was not until the percussion period that it could be successfully applied. There are several reasons why revolvers were not feasible in the flintlock and previous ignition eras. One was that the discharge of one load would often set off the other loads before the cylinders in the chamber came in line with the barrel. Another was the mechanical difficulty of producing accurate alignment between the barrel and the chamber to be fired. Both of these defects led to serious accidents and delayed the evolution of the revolver.

One of the rarest of all flintlock revolvers is that made by Elisha Collier, of Boston, Massachusetts, about 1820. American manufacturers were not interested in his invention, so he patented it in England in 1818, and in France in 1819; and it is known that he was active in making revolving pistols, rifled carbines, and fowling pieces about 1822. His was a true revolver type, with a chambered cylinder, but it was too far in advance of his time and is now known to only a few collectors. However, we mention its existence in the hope that you may some day be fortunate enough to find one for your collection.

Among the rarest guns in the world, the Cookson guns, both pistols and long arms, stand supreme, not only for their value and interest to collectors, but also because these guns in design and construction were far ahead of contemporary weapons of their period. These arms are repeating, breech-loading, magazine, flintlock firearms. The powder and bullets are held in separate chambers in the stock and successively conveyed to the barrel or pan by a revolving cylinder at the breech of the barrel, turned by a handle on an axis at right angles to that of the barrel. To load, the compartments are filled with powder and balls, without counting the balls or measuring the powder, for all this is provided by features incorporated in the design of this most unusual type of weapon. If spherical bullets weighing 250 grains are used, exactly ten rounds can be loaded and fired.

Two guns are known to be in existence bearing the marking "IOHN COOKSON FECIT" on the top of the barrel. In English, this can be translated roughly as "John Cookson Made." The two guns marked "IOHN COOKSON FECIT" were probably made in Boston, Mass., and advertised for sale there. They conform to a type made in England before and after 1800, but some authorities believe that the design originated in Italy about 1600.

There are in existence a few pistols and long arms utilizing the same principle as the Cookson. One is in the Birmingham, England, Museum, there is one in the Musée d'Artillerie at Paris, and there were four in the possession of Dr. S. Traner Buck, of Philadelphia. These are generally referred to by collectors as "Cookson type" firearms; they are exceedingly rare and valuable, and it is impossible to appraise accurately their dollars-and-cents worth, but they may be worth from $2,000 to $3,000 apiece, depending upon condition.

Another great rarity is the Ferguson Breech-Loading Flint-Lock Rifle, introduced in England, December 2, 1776, by Patrick Ferguson, who died, commanding the 71st Regiment, Second Battalion, of the Highland Light Infantry, in the battle of King's Mountain, South Carolina, October 7, 1780. It has been said that one hundred fifty to two hundred of his soldiers were armed with the rifle he developed; but after his death, some of the existing specimens were either lost by his own men or carried home as souvenirs by the victorious American forces. Only a few specimens are in the hands of collectors, and these are regarded as being very valuable. Strangely enough, the one in the Milwaukee Public Museum was found by Rudolph J. Nunnemacher in an obscure junk shop where he bought it for a price that was little more than its value as scrap iron!

It is possible that Cookson and Ferguson arms may be stored, this very minute, in old attics and barns where they were left by owners long since dead. One of you who read this book may be fortunate enough to discover one of these great rarities, and who knows, perhaps some new collector may stumble on the facts that will shed new light on the Cookson-type arms and other rarities.

The model years and descriptions of United States martial firearms given in this chapter are those commonly accepted by many beginning collectors and by some dealers. However, a detailed description of practically all of the U.S. martial firearms, together with their various model designations, and their values, is presented in the revised edition of *The Gun Collector's Handbook of Values*.

V

THE KENTUCKY RIFLE

———————

THE KENTUCKY RIFLE IS SO THOROUGHLY NATIVE TO THE United States that it is called the "American Rifle" by European authorities. True Kentucky flintlocks in their original condition are so much in demand that they command higher average prices than any other general type of weapon. Add to these facts the colorful historical associations of the Kentucky and you will understand why a Kentucky Rifle is one of the most highly prized guns in most American arms collections.

This was the weapon carried by George Washington's backwoodsmen when they saved four hundred British soldiers from certain slaughter by the Indians in the campaign waged by General Braddock against the French in our Colonial era. Firing from behind trees, with every shot aimed, Washington's men were able to pick off the Indians with rifles while the British soldiers, armed with the smoothbore "Brown Bess" and trained to fire in volleys from solid ranks, were being mowed down by the redskins.

Later, at the siege of Quebec, General Wolfe of the British Army placed in the front of his forces, for the advance to the "Plains of Abraham," companies of Pennsylvania Provincials armed with the Kentucky Rifle to act as "shock troops" against the French regulars. The accurate fire of these Americans drove back the advance guard of the French and cleared the way for the British regulars, with the result that Quebec was taken and Canada won for the British Crown.

In the American Revolution, to use the official phraseology of the British War Office: "The settlers from the backwoods of America used their hunting rifles with so much effect that the only effective rejoinder was to pit rifle against rifle; for this purpose Jägers were recruited on the Continent." These Jägers, it must be understood, were none other than the "Hessians" of our school histories. The old legend that King George III was unable to obtain Englishmen to fight against the American Revolutionists is all nonsense; the real reason for the use of the Hessians was that they were bought from the German rulers and could be used as soldiers at less expense than British subjects.

The Hessians played no great part in the War, but on the American side riflemen accounted for such victories as that of King's Mountain in 1780, where the British loss was four hundred killed and wounded to the American's eighty-eight. Losses such as these caused hot debates in the English Parliament and there were many suggestions for adopting rifles as military equipment; but it was not until 1794, eleven years after America had won its independence, that there was a single battalion of British soldiers armed entirely with the rifle.

The English army apparently forgot the lesson in rifle marksmanship taught them by the Americans in the Revolutionary War, for in the War of 1812 the bulk of the British soldiers were still using smoothbores. At the Battle of New Orleans, July 8, 1815, the British General Pakenham had 10,084 regulars opposing 3,918 Americans, most of whom were militiamen or recruits; but these Americans were armed with the Kentucky Rifle, which they fired from the protection of cypress logs and molasses barrels so accurately that the English lost a total of 3,336 dead and wounded as contrasted with a loss to General Andrew Jackson's force of only 8 killed and 13 wounded.

The Kentucky Rifle was not the official, regulation arm of the U.S. Army; instead, it was the private weapon of the hunters and marksmen who depended on it to obtain game and drive back the Indians, and although the Kentucky was the principal rifle of the flintlock period in America, comparatively few were bought by the United States for regular issue to troops.

As a fully developed arm, the Kentucky originated about the period 1725-1728, and it survived without much change until about 1830, when it was superseded by the percussion rifles and the breech-loaders which were just beginning to come into general use. Thousands of Kentucky Rifles were converted into percussion arms between 1830 and 1850, and this accounts for the scarcity of a true Kentucky type; but it is interesting to know that these converted Kentucky Rifles were used successfully on both sides of the Civil War, and there are records of even flintlock Kentuckies being carried by state troops in that War.

The name, "Kentucky," is a misnomer, which apparently arose about 1770 from the use of this rifle by the pioneers and settlers who were moving into the wilderness west of the Cumberland Mountains and east of the Mississippi River, a vast region called "Kentucky" long before that name was applied to a single state.

Actually, it should be called the "Pennsylvania Rifle,"

and some writers have begun to employ this term; for it was developed in Lancaster, Pennsylvania, by Swiss and German gunsmiths about 1725 to 1728. For many years arms historians believed that the Pennsylvania Rifle was developed from the typical Central European rifle of that period, carried by the men known as "Jägers" or "Chasseurs," but several experts now contend that the Pennsylvania (Kentucky) Rifle and the so-called Jäger type are cousins but not father and son.

In the two previous editions of *Gun Collecting,* the author expressed an unfavorable opinion of the Jäger type made in Germany, although he conceded that rifles of that period made in Switzerland were of good quality. Through years of research and the examination of many Jäger-type rifles it is now known that many of them were well made and comparatively accurate, but they did not meet the needs of Americans, hence the development of the Pennsylvania (Kentucky) Rifle.

The American pioneer wanted a rifle that was easily carried and fired, effective against both wild game and Indians, accurate at the usual ranges, capable of being loaded easily and swiftly with a few simple tools, easy to repair, and economical in the consumption of powder and lead, which not only cost money but added to the load the hunter often carried on expeditions hundreds of miles from any base of supplies.

In response to these demands, the German and Swiss gunmakers of Lancaster, Pennsylvania, reduced the caliber from about .70 to about .45; increased the average barrel length from about 31 to about 42 inches; made the trigger guard smaller and stronger; used curly maple for the stock; gave the rifle plain, open sights, both front and rear, fixed to the barrel by a grooved slide which permitted adjustment horizontally; and ornamented the rifle with an eight-pointed brass star sunk into the cheek-piece on the left side, this last feature being a strictly American idea which survived to the end of the Kentucky flintlock period. The barrel was made full octagon in cross-sectional shape. On the right side of the stock was placed a box, five inches long by one and one-half inches wide, covered with a hinged brass lid, in which the hunter could keep patches of tallow-greased buckskin. These patches were about the size of a dollar; wrapped around a bullet made a small fraction of an inch smaller than the bore, a greased patch enabled the shooter to load without the pounding required for the old German guns, thus cutting the loading time to about one fourth the number of seconds formerly consumed.

This description fits the average Kentucky in the early part of its history, but about 1790 the gunsmiths began to give the butt a distinct crescent shape, use imported locks, make the barrels longer, and employ a great deal of carving and silver or brass mounting; flat key pins for fastening the barrels to the stocks replaced the round ones of the early period. This fancier, but not necessarily better rifle, was popular until about 1830, when calibers were reduced to about .33, barrels were made shorter, and less attention was paid to the quality of the workmanship.

From about 1830 the Kentucky declined steadily in popularity until it almost disappeared as an important hunting arm about 1850, the reasons being that the Indians and wild game of any consequence were reduced in numbers, percussion rifles were now in general use, and the principal targets left for the flintlock, muzzle-loading Kentucky were squirrels and turkeys.

The collector wants an airtight description of the Kentucky so that he can always be sure of recognizing one of these beautiful, valuable, historical examples of American gunmaking genius; but it is impossible to give him a set of specifications which will always fit a Kentucky and not fit any other flintlock, muzzle-loading rifle. The reason is that Kentucky Rifles were handmade, by at least 500 different gunsmiths, none of whom ever turned out two rifles exactly alike in every detail. All we can do is to remember a few characteristics and then compare a weapon in question with one of the same supposed make, period, and type. For the beginning collector, the best advice is to study as many examples of true Kentuckies as he can find and then rely on the opinion of an honest expert.

Next to the actual examination of Kentuckians identified by collectors or dealers as true specimens, the best thing for the beginner to do is to read *The Kentucky Rifle,* by John G. W. Dillin, published in a revised edition in 1959 by George N. Hyatt, Wilmington, Delaware.

A third source of information is found in the catalogues and price lists of dealers in firearms for collectors, especially those which are illustrated with photographs of the rifles offered for sale. Here are a few examples, taken from various catalogues, which will show the details considered important by the dealers:

"Extremely rare and historical flintlock Kentucky by Sam Boone, nephew of Daniel Boone, who moved to Pennsylvania and started gunmaking in 1768. Barrel bears his signature and carries original browning. Total length 57″, with 42″ octagon barrel. Cal. 42, with 7 deep grooves. Ketland lock. There is a crack in the stock, but neatly and strongly mended. The stock itself is of fine tiger-flame maple mellowed by age with quite elaborate carving on the left side; silver moon on cheek piece: silver name plate on back of grip. The four pins that fasten barrel to stock go through into four silver half-moons. Very graceful deep carved stock with fine patch box."

The Boone Kentucky Rifle, as you will observe, fits the general description of the early type fairly well except for the rather elaborate silver decorations instead of the brass star; and although this usually indicates a later period, the available facts about the period in which Boone worked classes this particular rifle as a fairly early production. Its length, 57″, falls within the rather wide spread of early rifle lengths, which was from 51 to 77 inches.

You can readily understand that the fame of the Boone family adds to the value of this particular specimen, but even when the maker was known only as a gunsmith, a signed rifle is ordinarily worth more than one by an unknown maker. However, less than one half of the makers of Kentucky flintlocks marked their guns, and many of those who did merely put their initials on the barrel with a hard steel die. Even when you find a name, or initials, this may be the mark of the man who made the barrel but not the whole rifle, or it may be the stamp of a dealer; but the odds are in favor of its being the work of the riflemaker, since the number of men who made only barrels was small and few dealers branded their wares in that day.

Here is another excerpt from an arms catalogue:

"Kentucky flintlock by D. Boyer, of Orwigsburg, Pa., an

extensive maker of superposed and heavy match rifles. Over-and-under, 36-inch barrel. Curly maple stock, brass patch box, trigger guard and butt plate. Silver name on tang, and silver inlayed designs on forestock. Barrels revolve by hand. Patch box contains original screw type cleaning attachment for original hickory rod. Barrel marked 'D. Boyer'; lock plate marked '—Park, Warranted.' "

This Boyer rifle was "superposed," that is, one barrel was over the other; but rifles with barrels side-by-side were also made, the purpose of these double-barrel guns being to have one barrel rifled and the other smooth, so that it was available for either big or small game. We have described it for you principally to illustrate the fact that guns for a collector are often found with characteristics that do not fit the standard pattern.

A word of caution is now in order. Since most of the flintlock Kentucky Rifles were altered to percussion, the demand for the flintlock specimens has sometimes tempted unscrupulous persons to alter a percussion back to a flintlock for the purpose of increasing its value on sale to an unsuspecting customer. The cost of this alteration when a good job is done is about $25, and it is often done legitimately by gunsmiths for an owner who wants a flintlock as a fireplace decoration and not to deceive collectors; but a collector who really cares about obtaining a true Kentucky will not want an altered gun. Even an expert finds it difficult to recognize a skillful alteration; the reputation of the dealer is the beginner's best protection against deception.

Pennsylvania (Kentucky) flintlock rifles in 1960 averaged in value from $300 to $450, depending upon condition, but flintlocks altered to percussion sold from $100 to

$150, depending upon condition. Except for the ignition mechanism, one of these percussion Kentucky Rifles illustrates as well as the true type the graceful lines and deadly accuracy of the rifle that played an important part for a hundred years in the making of our history. Who knows, perhaps that humble percussion Kentucky you take as a second choice was carried by one of Andrew Jackson's men at New Orleans and then converted to do valiant duty in the Civil War.

The prices of firearms rise and fall with the purchasing power of the dollar, but the prices of Kentucky Rifles have risen higher than most other arms. The subject of Kentucky Rifle values is more fully discussed in *The Gun Collector's Handbook of Values*.

VI

PERCUSSION GUNS

O N NOVEMBER 11, 1663, SAMUEL PEPYS, THE FAMOUS English diarist, wrote this entry:

"At noon to the Coffee House, where, with Dr. Allen, some good discourse about physick and chymistry. And among other things I telling him what Dribble, the German Doctor, do offer of an instrument to sink ships; he tells me that which is more strange, that something made of gold, which they call in chymestry Aurum Fulminans, a grain, I think he said, of it put into a silver spoon and fired, will give a blow like a musquet, and strike a hole through the silver spoon downwards, without the least force upwards; and this he can make a cheaper experiment of he says with iron prepared."

The spelling and grammar in Pepys' diary may seem quaint, but the idea of the use of fulminates for explosive purposes is clear enough to show that the percussion principle is older than we commonly think. It was, however, delayed in practical application until the invention of the Reverend Alexander Forsyth, a Scotch Presbyterian Minister, of Belhelvie, in Aberdeenshire, who, in 1807, received a patent for a specially designed lock, in which a steel hammer or striker would explode a small quantity of detonating powder placed in the flashpan of the gun. Forsyth's invention, next to the discovery of gunpowder, was the

EARLY SHOULDER WEAPONS

TOP TO BOTTOM:
  2388, English Flintlock Blunderbuss
M-387, Japanese Matchlock Rifle
M-404, English Flintlock Blunderbuss
M-403, European Flintlock Blunderbuss
M-171, Italian Folding-Stock Percussion Blunderbuss, converted
        from flintlock
M-102, American, Wm. Lawrence Percussion Rifle-Pistol
M-456, American, J. Graves, Under-Hammer Percussion Rifle
M-229, Colt Dragoon, Model 1848, with Shoulder Stock
M-136, Starr Percussion Revolver, Stocked
M-497, Frank Wesson Pocket Rifle
Left: M-392, Japanese Matchlock
Right: M-390, Japanese Matchlock

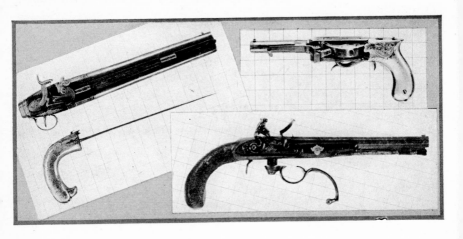

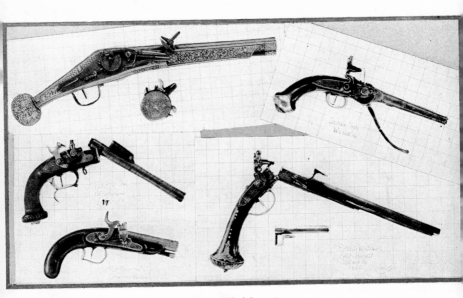

PLATE No. 6

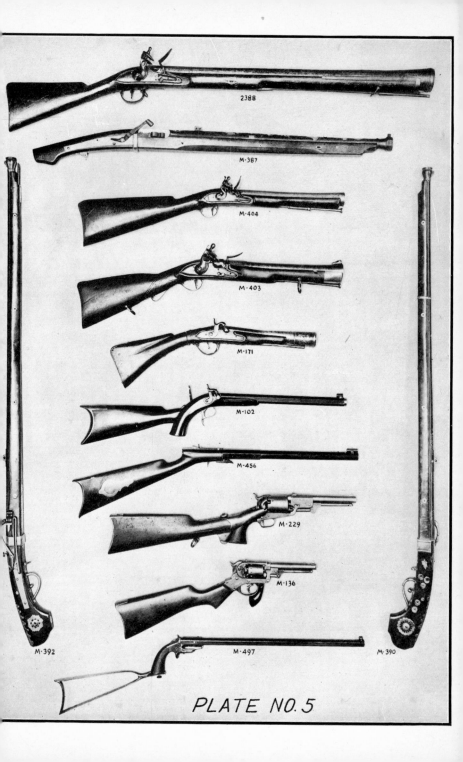

2388

M-387

M-404

M-403

M-171

M-102

M-456

M-229

M-136

M-392

M-390

M-497

PLATE NO. 5

GREAT RARITIES

Left: Double-barreled Percussion Stiletto pistol. Upper right: C. B. Allen "Cochran Pat." (side view). Lower right: Ferguson breech-loading flintlock pistol, introduced by Major (brevet Colonel) Patrick Ferguson, British Army. Ferguson rifles follow the same principle.

Upper left: Right side, ball-butt wheel lock pistol dated 1581. Center left: Forsyth Type breech-loading, Pottet, 1810. Lower left: Rev. Forsyth's original model. Upper right: Cookson type pistol, Wilson, 1820. Lower right: Breech-loading Snaphance, 1660.

most important discovery in the history of weapons, for it is the basic principle underlying the evolution of the metallic cartridge, the successful development of breech-loading, and all the other firearms improvements of today.

In 1812, Forsyth founded his own company, Forsyth & Co., in London. At least three types of Forsyth locks are recognized by the most advanced collectors, but the most interesting feature is his famous "Scent Bottle," one of the great rarities among guns. It gets its name from a magazine, shaped like a small flask or scent bottle, which holds a supply of the detonating powder. This scent bottle served a double purpose: the lower end held enough powder to prime twenty or thirty shots, while the upper end held a steel firing pin, through which the blow of the hammer was communicated to the priming in the enclosed pan.

This lock was extremely effective. It overcame the faults of the flintlock by being impervious to damp weather and heavy winds, at the same time giving a quicker and more complete ignition to the whole powder charge without the loss of powder through the vent. The only disadvantage of the new lock was that the priming was extremely sensitive. In fact, it was this great violence of the fulminates that had delayed the application of the percussion system to guns, for the force of the explosion had always scattered the powder before it had time to ignite the main charge. Forsyth's invention harnessed the force of the explosion to perform the useful function of ignition, but there was a danger that the percussion powder in the magazine might be exploded at the same time as the load in the bore. To guard against this accident, a safety plug was provided for the magazine; in case of a backfire, this plug would blow out and prevent the bursting of the magazine.

The Forsyth detonating principle was first regarded as dangerous and objectionable by the British Army; but sportsmen accepted it rapidly, and by 1825 other inventors had improved on the original lock enough so that the percussion cap came into general use on private arms. The British Army were still clinging to their old flintlock Brown Bess muskets; but the flintlocks could be converted to the new ignition system without much expense or trouble, so they accepted the percussion method officially in 1836. The Brown Bess muskets were all converted to percussion fire by 1842, and it is interesting to know that percussion rifles were first used in action by the British Second Border Regiment, at Amoy (now French Indo-China), on August 26, 1841. After much haggling by Parliament, the British government awarded Forsyth five thousand pounds sterling, paying the first installment to his widow on the day of his death, June 11, 1843.

In the United States, the percussion system was generally adopted by sportsmen about 1840, but the first regulation United States percussion pistol was the caliber .54 smoothbore of 1842, and the first regulation United States percussion rifle was the caliber .69 rifle, model 1842. However, it must be remembered that in 1842, both the United States and the British military firearms were still loaded from the muzzle, for the development of breech-loading had to wait for further improvements in the ignition method.

The first step in the development of the percussion system after Forsyth's use of loose powder was the introduction of the "PILL LOCK," sometimes called the "PELLET

LOCK," in which the detonating mixture was made into a ball or pill, sometimes enclosed in paper similar to that used in toy "cap-pistols." This avoided the objections to Forsyth's loose powder and was popular for several years in the United States and Continental Europe; but the English pill-lock guns have always been rare, the principal makers being Westley Richards and Joseph Manton. French pill locks are often found on revolvers with "turret"-shaped cylinders; among the American makers, probably the best example of a pill-lock arm is the target pistol made by William Billinghurst of Rochester, New York.

The second improvement was the "TAPE LOCK," an advanced form of pill lock in which the pellets were enclosed by or fastened to a long strip of paper or fabric, so that they could be successively fed to the firing position by the action of the lock. It must be observed, however, that the tape lock was not necessarily second in priority of invention, for it is credited by American authorities to Dr. Maynard, a dentist of Washington, D.C., who received his first patent in 1845. We mention it second here, because it logically comes after the pill lock. The Maynard tape primer was used by the United States in 1851 on Sharps and other rifles.

Third in point of logical development, but second in priority of time, was the invention of the "TUBE LOCK," patented by Joseph Manton, in England, in 1818. The name is derived from the fact that the basic principle is the use of a hollow copper tube, five-eighths of an inch long and one-sixteenth of an inch in outside diameter, and open at both ends. This tube was filled with a detonating compound containing fulminate of mercury and inserted in the vent of the gun, where it was held by a spring. At its outer and upper end it rested against a tiny anvil. A blow from the hammer exploded the contents and ignited the powder charge. Many guns with this tube-lock ignition were made in England by Joseph Manton, most of them being either fowling pieces or dueling pistols, and some were made as early as 1811.

Fourth in the progress of the percussion system was the "CAP LOCK," invented to overcome the chief fault of the tube lock, which was the tendency to blow the tubes out of the vents and permit the loss of power through the escape of powder gases at the breech. In the earlier form of the cap lock it was provided with a platinum disk, perforated to communicate with the breech and allow an escape of gas; but this was later found undesirable, and few guns made after 1835 are found with this feature.

The "cap" was a thimble-shaped cup holding a small quantity of detonating powder and placed on a hollow steel nipple leading to the powder charge. Captain Joshua Shaw, of Philadelphia, patented this cap in the United States for the first time in 1822, but he had previously applied for the patent in 1814. In the first form, the cap was made of iron; in 1815 he tried pewter; and in 1816 he perfected the copper cap, which was copied closely by all manufacturers from then until the close of the percussion era about fifty years later.

The beginner in gun collecting may not care a great deal about the exact date and the name of the inventor of the copper percussion cap, but among advanced collectors it has become quite a "tempest in a teapot." Nationally minded Americans generally give Captain Shaw the credit, while equally patriotic Britishers forget that the Captain was born a British subject and only became American by naturalization; in their natural desire to give one of their own people the glory, the British writers have sometimes advanced the names of Joseph Manton and Joseph Egg as the inventors of the cap. However, Charles Ffoulkes, the Master of Armouries of the Tower of London, said in his recent book, *Sword, Lance & Bayonet:*

"At first the detonating was effected by inserting small tubes or primers in place of Forsyth's somewhat elaborate magazines, and in or about 1836 a copper cap by Westley-Richards was introduced, *based on the previous invention of Captain Shaw of Philadelphia.*"

Regardless of who invented the copper cap, the fact remains that it made the percussion system the accepted method of ignition. Beginning about 1825, flintlocks were converted to percussion fire by several different ways of changing the mechanism. One method was to fit a screw plug into the vent; the plug contained the nipple and could be removed for cleaning. The original cock on the flintlock was removed and a hammer put in its place. This was simple and cheap; it caused the conversion of thousands of flintlocks in America and Europe and resulted in the shortage of fine flintlocks that collectors complain about today.

The United States, as we have already seen, adopted the percussion principle for its regulation martial arms about 1842. In considering guns of this period, we shall first mention the single-shot percussion pistols, followed by the revolvers and then the long arms. In using the term "martial," it is well to remember that it usually refers to arms actually bought and issued to troops by the Federal Government. Guns bought by individuals or by states are classed by collectors as "Secondary Martial Arms." They are of an infinite variety and open to dispute for lack of sufficient records.

The first regulation U.S. percussion pistol was the Model 1842, caliber .54, smoothbore, made by H. Aston, Middletown, Connecticut, I. N. Johnston of Middletown, Connecticut, and later by the Palmetto Armory, of Columbia, South Carolina. The latter make is the rarest, and is stamped "Palmetto Armory, S.C.," followed by 1852 on the lock plate. The barrel carries the year, the letters "P.V." (proof marks), the figure of a palm, and "Wm. Glaze & Co." The tang is dated 1853.

The Palmetto Armory was state-owned, but the machinery was installed by Glaze. Founded in 1852, it made arms for South Carolina until the Civil War, when it was run by the Confederacy.

Before the Model 1842 Pistol could be manufactured and delivered, the Model 1843 was issued to troops; therefore, it was the first regulation percussion pistol in service, even though the 1842 was designed first. This model is a .54 caliber smoothbore, and it is generally classed as a "box-lock" type because it has the hammer on the inside of the lock plate. Two firms made this pistol under contract to the government; these were N. P. Ames of Chicopee Falls, near Springfield, Massachusetts, and Henry Deringer, Jr., of Philadelphia. Their names appear on the guns, but you may also find "U.S.R.," the abbreviation for U.S. Revenue Service, as well as "U.S.N.," since this pistol was issued both to the Navy and to other services. It was carried extensively in the Mexican War.

The next government model was the U.S. Percussion Pistol-Carbine, Model 1855, called a pistol-carbine because it had a detachable shoulder stock so that it could be fired from either the hand or the shoulder. The stock is removed by pressing a button back of the trigger guard which releases a catch and frees the pistol. It was made at the Springfield Armory, and designed to use the Maynard tape primer. A few pattern models were probably made at Harpers Ferry. Specimens with the mark of "H. Aston & Co." are known, but they lacked the tape primer, being ordinary 1842 pistols with stocks. This weapon may have been used in the Civil War.

From January 1, 1861, to June 30, 1866, the United States bought 129,730 Colt Army Revolvers, 17,010 Colt Navy Revolvers; from Remington, 125,314 of the Army model, and 4,901 of the Navy model were purchased. In addition, the following makes and quantities were bought: Starr, 47,952; Le Faucheux, 12,375; Savage, 11,284; Whitney, 11,214; Roger & Spencer, 5,000; Pettingill, 2,001; Beall, 2,814; Joslyn, 1,100; Allen, 536; Adams, 415; and Perrin, 200. This gives a fair idea of the variety of makes.

Turning from short to long arms, we find that the first U.S. regulation shoulder arms were the Model 1842 Percussion Musket, caliber .69, and the Model 1842 Percussion Rifle, caliber .54; both of these are also known to collectors as the Model 1841. This matter of Model years causes a little confusion for the beginner, but you can avoid a lot of worry by taking the designations "on faith." The years are supposed to be the ones in which the government accepted the pattern for a model and officially authorized its production. They are not necessarily the years in which production started. For instance the 1842 Musket was first made at Springfield in 1844, and at Harpers Ferry in 1845.

The 1842 Musket was the last of the regulation smoothbores, it was the first regulation percussion firearm, and the first weapon to be produced in quantities under the completely interchangeable plan, whereby the parts from one gun would fit another without alteration. Like the Musket, the 1842 Rifle marked the passing of the flintlock era and the beginning of the percussion period. The Rifle was recognized internationally as the most accurate military rifle using a spherical bullet, a supremacy it held until the cone-shaped bullet was adopted with the Model of 1855. This 1842 Rifle was used for big-game hunting, in the Indian Wars, the War with Mexico, and even during the Civil War. Because of its accuracy it was sometimes called the "Yerger," a corruption of the German word Jäger, referring to a member of a rifle team or a member of a rifle regiment of that name. It was also called the "Harpers Ferry Rifle" because most of the government-made specimens came from that armory. "The Mississippi" and also Model 1841 are other names.

With the adoption of a cone-shaped bullet, the government issued a new model, that of 1855, made in two sizes, the longer being called a Percussion Rifle Musket, while the shorter was known as the Percussion Rifle. Both are caliber .58, and they are easily recognized by the presence of the Maynard Tape Priming Magazine. The tape was waterproofed and contained patches of fulminate distributed at regular intervals. The tape was coiled in a cavity in the

A VARIETY OF SHOULDER WEAPON TYPES

Top to Bottom:

M-381, German Wheel Lock Rifle, Circa 1675

M-413, English Double-Barrel Flintlock Shotgun

M-530, Spanish Presentation Single-Barrel Percussion Shotgun

M-551, German Sporting Needle Gun

M-523, Ancient Hungarian Air-Rifle, Operated by Bellows and Spring

M-464, American, M. F. Crandall, Percussion 3-Barrel Rifle-Shotgun

M-536, English, 4-Barrel Percussion Shotgun

M-501, American, Combination Rifle and Shotgun

M-461, American Percussion Rifle, Super-Posed Barrels

M-462, American, Golcher 4-Barrel Percussion Rifle

M-548, Belgian Magazine-Fed Saloon Rifle

M-500, American, A. D. Perry Percussion Sporting Rifle

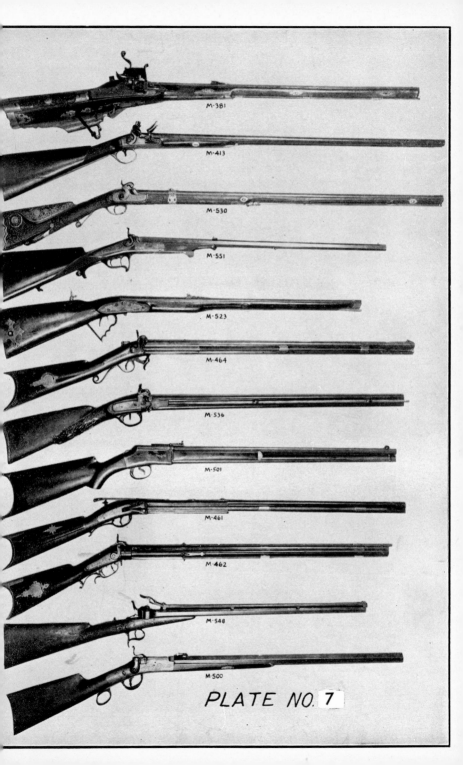

M-381

M-413

M-530

M-551

M-523

M-464

M-536

M-501

M-461

M-462

M-548

M-500

PLATE NO. 7

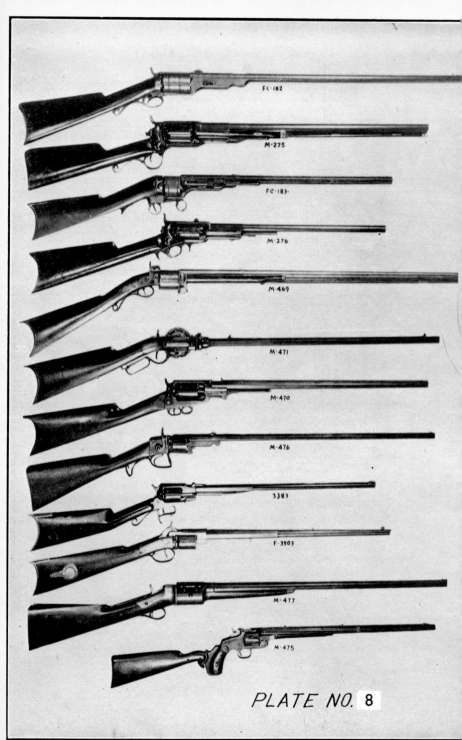

FC-182

M-275

FC-183

M-276

M-469

M-471

M-470

M-476

3383

F-3503

M-477

M-475

PLATE NO. 8

REVOLVING RIFLES, SHOTGUNS
AND CARBINES

FC-182, Paterson Colt Percussion Revolving Hammer-Shotgun

M-275, Colt's Revolving Percussion Shotgun

FC-183, Paterson Colt Percussion Revolving Hammerless Carbine

M-276, Colt's Presentation Percussion Revolving Rifle

M-469, American, E. S. Ormsby Pill-Lock Revolving Rifle

M-471, P. W. Porter Percussion Turret Rifle

M-470, J. L. Wyler Revolving Percussion Rifle

M-476, English Revolving Percussion Rifle, patented by Thomas Pennell, 1853

3383, Remington Revolving Percussion Carbine

F-3503, American, Warner Revolving Percussion Rifle

M-477, American, Roper Repeating Percussion Shotgun

M-475, Smith & Wesson Revolving Rifle

lock plate, fed into position, and fired by a blow from the hammer which at the same time cut off the used portion. When damp, the tape was useless, but the gun could be used with percussion caps. Both the Rifle and the Rifle Musket mark the beginning of rifled arms and the passing of the smoothbore, none of the latter being made after 1856. The Rifle was made at Harpers Ferry, which was destroyed in April, 1861; so rifles marked 1861 are rare and much desired by collectors.

The Model 1861 Percussion Rifled Musket, caliber .58, was practically the same as the rifle musket of 1855, except that the Maynard primers were omitted, and there were slight changes in the design of the rear sight and ramrod. Historians have called this model "the principal infantry weapon of the Civil War." Between 1861 and the end of 1864, the government made more than 800,000 at the Springfield Armory and bought about 700,000 from private contractors.

To supplement the arms of American manufacture, the government bought nearly one-half million English Enfield Percussion Rifled Muskets, Model 1853, caliber .577, and the Confederacy bought nearly as many. This musket took the American caliber .58 bullet, and was probably the best of the many foreign arms bought for the war.

The U.S. Model 1863 Rifle Musket, caliber .58, closely resembles the Model 1861 Rifle Musket; but if the two are observed, side by side, you will see that the 1863 Model has a case-hardened lock plate, the hammer is "S"-shaped, there are oval bands, the swell in the ramrod is omitted, and there is an improved rear sight. It was made at Springfield, and also by private contractors.

Eli Whitney, Jr., the son of the Eli Whitney who invented the cotton gin, made the U.S. Whitneyville Percussion Navy Rifle, caliber .69, at Whitneyville, Connecticut, and delivered 10,000 in 1863 for the Navy. The outstanding peculiarity is the large caliber in comparison with the usual caliber .58 which had been used since 1855.

The Remington company furnished the U.S. government with the U.S. Model 1863 Remington Percussion Rifle, caliber .58; from May 31, 1864, to March 24, 1866, 39,000 were delivered for the Army, but it is not certain that any of these were actually used in the Civil War.

An important piece for any collection is the U.S. Model 1864 Percussion Rifle Musket, caliber .58, because it was the last of the regulation muzzle-loaders made for the armed forces of the United States. The value of breech-loading had been realized by the ordnance officers for many years, but the outbreak of the Civil War had prevented a change from muzzle-loading to breech-loading which would have required designing and making new machinery.

After the battle of Gettysburg, which was fought on the first three days of July, 1863, a shipment of 37,574 arms were picked up from the battlefield and sent to Washington, D.C. Of this number, 24,000 were found fully loaded. One fourth of these loaded guns had only one load in the barrel, but one half had two loads, and the remaining 6,000 arms had from three to ten loads in each gun.

Some of the muskets were loaded with the paper cartridges upside down so that the powder was not exposed to the ignition. One musket was found with twenty-three loads in the barrel, some right side up and some upside down. From all this evidence of the excitement prevailing during the battle, the government authorities estimated that one third of the soldiers on each side were ineffective as fighting men. With a breech-loading arm, this multiple loading would be impossible; the soldier would have to fire one round before loading another into the chamber. Our government had learned its lesson; the Civil War marked the end of the muzzle-loader, and it also marked the close of the percussion era, for it was the development of the metallic cartridge that made possible the sealing of the breech against loss of power from the escape of powder gas.

Thousands of men, released from the Union and Confederate armies, sought their fortunes in the new lands opened for settlement in the West. Many of them took with them the percussion muskets, rifles, and revolvers that they had carried through the war. These were used for hunting, for fighting the Indians, and to enforce the rude justice of the frontier. Few could afford the cartridge guns when they were first introduced, and they clung to the guns they knew, the firearms based on the invention of the Reverend Forsyth so many years before.

A more detailed discussion of percussion arms of all types is given in *The Gun Collector's Handbook of Values* and in *Guns of the Old West*.

VII

SAMUEL COLT AND
HIS PERCUSSION REVOLVERS

———————

MORE THAN A CENTURY AGO A SIXTEEN-YEAR-OLD American seaman, bound for Calcutta on the Brig *Corvo,* sat watching the revolving spokes on the ship's steering wheel. No matter which way the wheel turned, right or left, each spoke came directly in line with a clutch which held it fast. The youngster saw in this mechanism an idea which could be used in designing a repeating gun. Out of a discarded tackle block he carved a model. Previous revolving-cylinder guns operated by hand, but the seaman's invention was the first practical revolving gun with automatic revolution and cylinder locking, operated by cocking the hammer. This is the legend started by Colt.

The seaman-inventor was Samuel Colt. Born in Hartford, Connecticut, July 19, 1814, his boyhood was one of poverty and hard work on a farm and in a factory; but he had dreams of success, and by his genius, perseverance, and personality he made those dreams come true. The word "Colt" today is more than the name of an inventor; it is a synonym for "revolver," a weapon that was used in the Mexican War, the Civil War, the Spanish-American War, the Filipino Insurrection, the World Wars, and the battles with the Indians in the conquest of the West. It has been carried by saints and sinners, heroes and cowards, bankers and gamblers, soldiers and sailors, cowboys and rustlers, and all the other colorful characters who have contributed their lives to the pageant of American history.

At the age of eleven, while working on the farm, Sam Colt found a book which told about inventions, the construction of the galvanic battery and the making of gunpowder. These subjects interested him so much that he decided to experiment for himself. A year later he made a galvanic battery and used it to fire gunpowder at a distance, but the result was too tame; by waterproofing the electric wires he was able to explode gunpowder under water. To demonstrate his discovery, he placed a charge under a raft on a pond near Ware, Massachusetts, and blew it "sky high." The only immediate result was a protest from the neighbors, but this experiment eventually led to the issuance of United States patents for the first submarine telegraph cable and the battery used for submarine harbor defense.

Sam's grandfather, Major John Caldwell, a veteran of the Revolutionary War, gave the boy a horse pistol and thrilled him with stories of men who had marched with Washington; but Sam's favorite tale concerned Tim Murphy and his double-barreled rifle. In an effort to design a repeater, the lad tied four gun barrels together and revolved them so that each in turn would be fired by the same lock. This plan failed when all four barrels went off at the same time; and it was not until 1830, when he shipped before the mast, that he found in the steering wheel the solution to his problem, according to legend.

Actually, the basic idea of a revolver probably did not

originate with Colt. What he did was to make the revolver a commercially successful weapon, just as Henry Ford did not invent the automobile but was the first to produce it in quantity at a reasonable price. In order to make money, Colt toured the country under the name of "Dr. Coult," giving lectures on chemistry accompanied by demonstrations of the effect of laughing gas.

In 1832, Colt sent a description of his basic idea to the United States Patent Office. In 1833 he constructed, with money saved from his lecture trips, both a pistol and a rifle on the principle for which he obtained French and English patents in 1835, when he visited Europe. On his return to the United States, he received his first American patent, February 25, 1836. On March 5, 1836, he formed the Patent Arms Manufacturing Co., at Paterson, New Jersey, at the foot of the falls of the Passaic River where he could obtain water power to run the machinery.

Here at Paterson were made the famous revolvers, revolving rifles, and revolving shotguns so highly regarded by gun collectors. There are a number of models with the Paterson mark; they include various types, calibers, and barrel lengths, but the most famous was the Texas Paterson revolver, .36 caliber, five-shot, with a concealed trigger, with a 7.5 inch barrel.

This revolver has been known as the "Texas" model by reason of its popularity among the Texans in their war for independence against Mexico. It was one of the first Colts that could be fired from one hand, and it is distinguished from all subsequent models and types by the concealed folding trigger which snaps out when the gun is brought to the full cock. Although the Colt company of today lists the

COLTS THAT MADE HISTORY

LEFT COLUMN:

F 5220, English Colt Dragoon Model 1848
F 5436, U.S. Colt Dragoon Model 1848
F 5358, Colt Army Model 1860, Full Fluted Cylinder
F 5054, Confederate Colt Navy Revolver
F 5560, Belgian Colt Navy Model Revolver
F 5406, Belgian Colt Navy Model 1851
F 5412, Colt's Navy Model 1851, Cut for Shoulder Stock
F 5095, Colt's Navy Model 1851

RIGHT COLUMN:

F 4024, Colt Belt Model 1862, Half-Fluted and Rebated Cylinder
F   577, Colt Pocket Model 1853
F 5302, Colt Pocket Model 1849
F 5096, Colt's Pocket Model 1848
F 5211, Colt's Model 1849, sometimes called "Wells Fargo"
F 3783, Colt Side-Hammer Model 1855
F 5041, Colt Side-Hammer Model 1855
M 248, Colt Side-Hammer Model 1855, Full Fluted Cylinder
F 5549, Belgian Colt Pocket Model Revolver

CENTER:

F 5131, Shoulder Stock for Colt Dragoon Model 1848

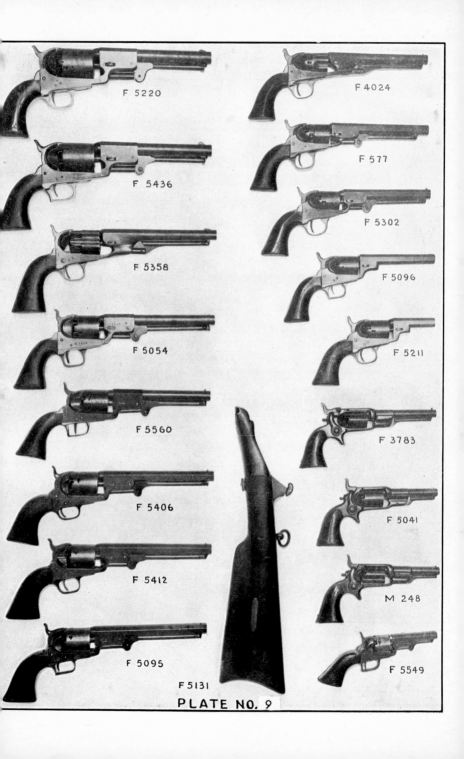

F 5220

F 4024

F 5436

F 577

F 5358

F 5302

F 5054

F 5096

F 5560

F 5211

F 5406

F 3783

F 5412

F 5041

M 248

F 5095

F 5131

F 5549

PLATE NO. 9

F 5066

F 5365

F 5121

F 5328

F 5216

F 5194

F 5221

F 5087

F 5200

F 5098

F 5122

F 5089

PLATE NO. 10

PERCUSSION REVOLVERS OF THE CIVIL WAR

LEFT COLUMN:

F 5066, Wesson & Leavitt Percussion Army Revolver
F 5121, Allen & Wheelock Percussion Navy Revolver
F 5216, Butterfield Percussion Army Revolver
F 5221, Savage First Model Navy Revolver, Figure-8 Guard
F 5200, Starr Presentation Army Revolver
F 5122, Joslyn Civil War Percussion Army Revolver

RIGHT COLUMN:

F 5365, Freeman Percussion Army Revolver
F 5328, Allen & Wheelock Percussion Army Revolver
F 5194, J. F. Garrett & Co., Greensboro, N. C., Confederate Percussion Pistol
F 5087, Lemat Percussion Civil War Revolver
F 5098, Pettingill Percussion Army Revolver
F 5089, Springfield Arms Co. Percussion Revolver, single-trigger, 1850 Model

caliber .36 as typical, calibers from .28 to .40, both inclusive, are in existence, and specimens are found with barrels as long as twelve inches. Two types of stocks are recognized by collectors, one called the "Paterson," which was the usual kind furnished with the gun, and another called the "Straight Stock." These and many other technical details do not interest the collector in the beginning, but they furnish a wide field for study as he becomes more advanced in his hobby.

Greatly coveted by Colt collectors is the Whitneyville-Walker, Model 1847, named for Captain Sam Walker of the Texas Rangers who, according to tradition, conferred with Colt, pointed out defects in the Texas Model, and suggested improvements. The result was a heavy .44 caliber six-shooter provided with an attached lever for ramming the bullets into the chamber of the cylinders, and a fixed trigger guard.

The Whitneyville-Walker, Model 1847, was made at Whitneyville, Conn., and is also called Colt Army Revolver, Model 1847; Colt-Walker Model 1847; Whitneyville Walker, and Walker Pistol. It is a single-action. The 9-inch round barrel has an octagonal breech. The total length is 15.5 inches. The straight round cylinder is usually found engraved with a scene of battle between Indians and U.S. dragoons.

Paterson Colt revolvers were described in early Colt advertisements as Pocket Pistols, Belt Pistols, and Holster Pistols. Pocket pistols are normally .28, .31, or .34 caliber; and their barrel lengths are usually 2.5, 3, 3.5, 4, 4.5, or 4.75 inches. Belt pistols are normally either caliber .31 or caliber .34 and the barrel lengths usually range between

4 and 6 inches. Holster pistols are all caliber .36 and the barrel lengths are 4, 4.5, 5, 5.5, 6, 7.5, 9, and 12 inches but most are either 7.5 or 9 inches long.

Colt made rifles, carbines, and shotguns (with the typical revolving cylinder used in his hand guns) at Paterson. The U.S. government bought 50 carbines or rifles for a campaign against the Seminole Indians in Florida, in 1838. Although comparatively few martial shoulder arms were made at Paterson, and they are considered great rarities, existing specimens have seldom brought prices as high as those paid for the Paterson revolvers, thus illustrating the fundamental rule of arms valuation that demand, and not rarity, is the primary factor in creating values.

The Paterson Colt Model 1839 Carbine was tested at the government's Dragoon School of Practice, Carlisle Barracks, Pennsylvania, in 1841, and 160 were purchased. The tests had something to do with the order, but the deciding matter was the experience of the Army officers with the early model in the Seminole War. There they had found that the Seminole Indians would approach the soldiers, draw their fire, and then swoop down and massacre them before they could reload their old single-shot pistols. Armed with the Colt, the soldiers could defeat the Indians without any difficulty. These trials encouraged Colt to think that he could obtain government contracts for all of his guns; but a combination of economy by the politicians and conservatism by the Army officers blasted his hopes. An economic depression arrived; there were quarrels among the officers of the corporation; and sales were few. As a consequence, the company failed in 1841 and operations ceased in 1842.

Disheartened, Samuel Colt spent the next five years in continuing his experiments with the galvanic battery where he had left off after the explosion of the raft, and he developed his waterproof cable to the extent that he was able to present the United States with a submarine mine for harbor defense. Congress showed its appreciation by appropriating $20,000 for further experiments. The boyhood pranks were now recognized as scientific achievements, but Colt appreciated most the newspaper headlines which made him known nationally and gave him a prestige he needed for the sale of his revolvers.

The outbreak of the Mexican War gave him a chance to capitalize on his publicity. Texas Rangers joined the forces of General Zachary Taylor, taking with them their own mounts and equipment, including the already famous "Texas" Model Colt Revolver. The Texans were brave fighters with any equipment, but General Taylor was particularly impressed by their ability to deliver a withering fire from their revolvers that sent the Mexican line reeling back, time after time. Determined to have the latest weapons for his men, Taylor sent an order for 1,000 Colt Revolvers.

"WANTED: A Colt six-shooter to use as a model." This is the advertisement that Colt is said to have inserted in newspapers when he received the government order, but it is probably only a myth. For several years he made few or no guns. According to the legend, he had no revolver to copy for the new order.

According to tradition, Colt received suggestions for the design of the Whitneyville Walker, Model 1847, from Captain Samuel Walker, who had come from Texas to speed up delivery. Since Colt now had no factory of his own, he contracted with Eli Whitney to make the revolvers according to Colt's specifications. Although the Model 1847 is marked "Address Sam'l Colt, New York City" on the barrel, there was no factory in New York. This marking was intended to give prestige to Colt.

After the manufacture of the Whitneyville Walker, Model 1847, Colt moved in 1848 to what he regarded as his home town, Hartford, Connecticut, and all Colt arms thereafter were made there. First in importance of the Hartford models was the Colt Army Revolver, Model 1848, also known as the Improved Holster Pistol, the Old Model Holster Pistol, the Old Model Army Pistol, Model of 1848 Holster Pistol, the Dragoon Colt, and the No. 1 Dragoon. This percussion revolver is caliber .44, 6-shot, single-action, with a 7.5-inch round barrel, octagonal at rear, and rifled with seven grooves. The total length is 14 inches and the weight is 4 lbs. 1 oz. The cylinder is usually found engraved with a scene of a battle between soldiers and Indians. The octagonal part of the barrel is marked on top "Address Sam'l Colt, New York City."

Specialists in the Model 1848 recognize three principal variations, modifications, or models, as you may be pleased to call them:

1. Square-back trigger guard. Rounded cylinder-stop recesses. Vertical loading-lever latch.
2. Trigger guard usually oval but sometimes square-backed, as before. Rectangular cylinder-stop recesses. Loading-lever latch is horizontal instead of vertical.
3. Has a two-leaf rear sight and is cut for a shoulder stock.

In addition to other markings, cylinders are sometimes engraved "U.S. Dragoons" or "U.S. Navy" instead of the usual "U.S.M.R." or "U.S.M.I."

The Colt Model 1848 Percussion Pocket Revolver, caliber .31, 5 shots, was also an early Hartford model, made with barrel lengths from three to six inches, with a removable cylinder, a square trigger guard, and no loading lever; but the latter feature was added later. The Colt company, in their book, *A Century of Achievement* (1936), state that this Model 1848 was the one adopted by the Wells Fargo Express Company for their messengers; this may be true, but the Wells Fargo Company was not founded until 1852, and collectors usually consider that the Colt Model of 1849, without a loading lever, was the true Wells Fargo type. Both may be correct, for the express messengers were not issued one standard revolver model; they carried several makes, models, calibers, and barrel lengths.

The Colt Model 1849 Percussion Pocket Revolver was another weapon that was popular in its day, and still liked by collectors. It must not be inferred that a model was discontinued when a later one was produced, for such was not the case. This Model of 1849, for instance, was made in Hartford from 1849 to 1873, and in London from 1853 to 1857. The Model 1849 was caliber .31, but it is difficult to lay down any definite rules about the Colt Percussions; he made his arms in an infinite variety of calibers and barrel lengths, and the same model might be made with either 5 or 6 chambers in the cylinder. To make matters more interesting for the collector, just when you think you have acquired a complete collection of even one model, someone turns up with a custom-made Colt, usually a presentation piece, which violates all the previously known facts.

Colt made various types of shoulder arms at Hartford, but the big demand was for revolvers. Colt's star seemed to rise in the West. Gold was discovered in 1849, and the resulting trek toward the setting sun sent thousands of Easterners over the plains, armed with Colt revolvers, and often guarded by mounted soldiers who carried Dragoon Revolvers in pairs in the holsters attached to their saddles. Traders, too, carried Colts, not only for self-protection, but also for sale, since a Colt purchased in the East for a comparatively small sum often could be sold in the West for a much higher price because of the high regard the pioneers had for Colt products.

The most popular percussion revolver among the plainsmen was the Colt Model 1851 Navy Revolver, caliber .36. On the cylinder is a picture of a naval battle and the words "Engaged 16 May 1843." According to some historians, this represented an engagement between a ship manned by Mexicans and one by Texans fighting for their independence, but the ship may have been the United States Ship *Mississippi,* the first United States steam warship to engage in battle.

The year 1851 marked not only the issuance of new Colt models, but also his trip to Europe where he visited the rulers, laid plans for opening a London factory, and came back to Hartford with orders for guns from the nations preparing for the Crimean War. The London factory began to manufacture guns in 1853 and did not close until 1857. Navy and Pocket Models were made in the London plant;

these are *stamped* on the barrel with a die, "ADDRESS:— COL. COLT. LONDON."

Colt tried to introduce ideas of mass production in London, making the parts of one gun interchangeable with the parts of any other gun of the same model; but he encountered the opposition of the trade guilds, who opposed any progress in manufacturing efficiency on the grounds that the use of machines threw men out of employment. They brought pressure on the public officials and caused no end of trouble; but in spite of these difficulties the London factory furnished the Viceroy of Egypt with 5,000 revolvers and supplied the British government with 200,000 for use in the Crimean War.

Back in America, in 1855, Colt obtained a charter for his organization under its present name, Colt's Patent Fire Arms Manufacturing Company; established the world's largest private armory in new quarters in Hartford; and developed a new revolver called the "Side Hammer Model," also referred to as the "Model 1855." It had a jointless frame with a top strap to which the barrel was attached, a hammer on the side, and the cylinder pin was now removable from rear instead of the front.

The list of models, calibers, and sizes of revolvers, rifles, carbines, and shotguns made by Colt is a long one. Samuel Colt was constantly experimenting with new ideas, launching new models, and improving on the older types. He was probably too busy as an inventor, manufacturer, and salesman-de-luxe, to stop long enough to record every gun turned out by his factory. To make matters worse, a great fire destroyed some of the Colt documents in 1864. Instead of discouraging collectors, this lack of certainty adds to the enjoyment of specializing in Colts, for some new variation is found each year, thus adding to our store of knowledge.

From the Model 1855, collectors usually jump to the Models 1860, 1861, and 1862, because these are in the "martial" class, that is, they were used in the Civil War. During that conflict, the Colt Armory produced and sold to the government 69,655 revolvers in 1861; 111,676 in 1862; 136,579 in 1863; and 69,107 during 1864 and 1865. At the same time they supplied the government with 113,980 rifled muskets, and nearly 7,000 rifles.

The Model 1860 Percussion Army Revolver is .44 caliber and weighs two pounds, eleven ounces; the Model 1861 Percussion Navy is .36 caliber, with a round barrel and weighs two pounds, ten ounces. The Model 1862 Percussion Belt Revolver is .36 caliber. There were slight variations in all three of these models for barrel length and weight; but collectively they are classed by collectors as "New Model Percussion" and distinguished from previous models by a round barrel and a ratchet loading lever.

Samuel Colt was one of the few men who foresaw the coming of the Civil War; he enlarged his factory, installed additional machinery, and made his estimates on a basis of one million Union soldiers fighting for a period of five years! History has shown how accurate was his prediction. Without regard to his own health, he put his whole body and soul into the Federal cause and worked so hard that he died on January 10, 1862, *at the age of forty-eight,* right at the prime of his life. For three days he lay in state, and on the fourth day he was buried with the full military honors of his rank, a Lieutenant Colonel of the Connecticut Militia. To the slow tap of muffled drums, troops with reversed arms followed his casket to the grave between the long double lines of bareheaded employees of the company he had founded.

Gun collectors who want to specialize in Colt weapons will find that all the types, models and variations are described and valued in the latest edition of *The Gun Collector's Handbook of Values*. Since the author of *Gun Collecting* wrote the first edition of 1939 and the first revised edition of 1947, there has been a vast amount of detailed research which has resulted in the publication of several excellent books on Colt arms. These are listed in the Bibliography and should be studied carefully by those who want to know the story behind their weapons.

Cartridge arms in general, including some of the most interesting Colt cartridge weapons, are discussed in the next chapter.

VIII

CARTRIDGE GUNS

———————

$\mathbf{T}$HE DEVELOPMENT OF CARTRIDGE GUNS IS A SECOND period in the percussion era because both the percussion and the cartridge systems owe their origin to Forsyth's practical application of fulminates to the firing of the powder charge; but breech-loading was not practical until the introduction of the metallic cartridge containing its own ignition. The early percussion breechloaders generally used a charge of powder wrapped with a ball or a conical bullet in a paper envelope, but it did not contain the means of ignition. It was fired externally, and whether the detonating powder was loose, or inside a cap, tube, or tape, the primer was still separate from the cartridge. It is true that the paper envelope was often chemically treated so that it would burn quickly, but smoldering sparks sometimes remained in the chamber and set off the next charge before the shooter pulled the trigger. To overcome this defect, to provide a better gas check, and to increase the ease of loading, extracting, and ejecting, the metallic cartridge was evolved. It went through several stages; these are generally classed as: Needle Gun, Pin-Fire, Center-Fire, and Rim-Fire.

Dreyse, a German gunsmith, is usually credited with the invention of the needle gun, which he patented in 1838, although sticklers for the truth insist that Dreyse stole the

REMINGTON REVOLVERS AND PISTOLS

LEFT COLUMN:
F 5247, Remington Army Revolver
F 5350, Remington Double-Action Navy Revolver
F 5730, Remington Full Fluted Cylinder Percussion Revolver
F 3346, Remington Frontier Revolver
F 5926, "Rolling-Block" Army Pistol
F 5147, Navy Pistol
F 5219, Spur-Trigger Navy Pistol
F 5176, Remington-Elliot Single-Shot Derringer

CENTER COLUMN:
F 5199, Remington 3rd Model Beals Pocket Percussion Revolver,
    4-inch barrel
M 303, Remington-Smoot Revolver, .38 Cal., rubber grips
F 3411, Remington-Smoot Revolver, .32 Cal., ivory grips
F 4999, New Line Cartridge Revolver
F 4041, Remington Percussion Pocket Model Revolver
F 5418, Vest Pocket Pistol
F 5250, Vest Pocket Pistol

RIGHT COLUMN:
F 2945, .46 Caliber Army Conversion
F 5415, Belgian-Remington Pistol
F 5432, Remington 1st Model Derringer
F 5379, Remington-Rider Magazine Pistol
M 158, Remington 1st Model Beals Pocket Percussion Revolver,
    3-inch barrel
F 5280, Remington-Elliot Derringer, 4-shots
F 5092, Zig-Zag Derringer
F 5140, Ring-Trigger Derringer, Remington-Elliot, 5-shots
F 5165, Remington-Rider Percussion Revolver
F 5334, Vest Pocket Pistol

F 5247

F 2945

F 5350

F 5415

F 5432

F 5730

F 5199

F 5379

F 3346

M 303

M 158

F 5926

F 3411

F 5280

F 5092

F 5147

F 4999

F 5140

F 4041

F 5165

F 5219

F 5176

F 5418

F 5250

F 5334

PLATE NO. 11

F 5978

F 5448

M 2181

F 1285

F 6152

F 5440

F 5446

F 5441

F 5442

F 5447

PLATE NO. 12

CASED PISTOLS AND REVOLVERS

LEFT COLUMN:

F 5978, Colt London Navy Model 1851 Cased Pair

M 2181, Pair Westley Richards English Percussion Pistols, Cased

F 6152, Mortimer-English Flintlock Holster Pistols, Cased

F 5441, Hollis English Percussion Revolver, Cased

RIGHT COLUMN:

F 5448, Colt English Pocket Model 1849, Cased

F 1285, Kent & Co. English Cased Pair Flint-Lock Great-Coat Pistols

F 5440, Tranter English Percussion Revolver, Cased

F 5446, American Percussion Pistol, Cased

F 5447, Wm. Marston 1st Model Dagger Cartridge Pistol, Cased

F 5442, Frank Wesson Vest-Pocket Pistol, Case Not Original

idea from Pauly, a Swiss, who first applied this method to fowling pieces in 1812. As a collector, you may wonder why it is important to know who invented a gun and where it was first made. This is necessary because you may be fortunate enough to find a gun produced by an original inventor; if you are not familiar with at least a few of the historical facts, you might overlook an opportunity to acquire a rare and valuable specimen for your collection.

The Dreyse needle guns were bolt-action, breech-loading arms, fired by means of a steel needle which pierced the base of the cartridge, traveled through the whole powder charge, and then passed through a papier-mâché wad to strike the detonating pellet located between the wad and the bullet. The chief defects were the escape of gas at the breech, the deterioration of the needle by corrosion or bending, and the lack of any means of extraction. In spite of its faults, the Prussian Army adopted the Dreyse in 1842 and used it in their wars with Denmark, Austria, and France. The Dreyse is interesting to collectors as the grandfather of all modern, bolt-action rifles.

The true pin-fire system of ignition was invented by Houiller, a French gunsmith, in 1847; but it was improved in 1854 by Le Faucheux, another Frenchman, who popularized the pin-fire in his own invention, the "drop-down," hinged barrel breechloader, which still survives in our modern single- and double-barrel shotguns. In its fully developed form, the pin-fire cartridge has a primer or cap inside the metal case; and a little pin which looks like a short nail sticks out of the side. In the breech of the rifle barrel, or the cylinder of a revolver, there is a slot for this pin to protrude through; when the hammer hits the pin, it drives the pin downward and into the cartridge, where it discharges the cap and fires the powder charge. Accidental discharge of a pin-fire cartridge takes place very easily and is a source of danger. This type of ignition is still used in Continental Europe, especially France; the best example of the pin-fire for the collector is the Le Faucheux revolver used by both sides in our Civil War.

The rim-fire cartridge was a logical evolution of the percussion cap. It was first made by Flobert, of Paris, some time between 1835 and 1846. The first revolving arm for the rim-fire cartridge was the Smith & Wesson revolver using the .22 short cartridge, patented in 1855. The cartridge is merely a short copper tube, closed at one end, with a bullet at the other end and powder in between. The closed end is flat, with a hollow rim; inside the rim there is a layer of the detonating mixture. When fired, the firing pin or the nose of the hammer, as the case may be, strikes this rim, crushing in the detonator at the point of impact, and causing it to ignite the powder charge. Rim-fire cartridges are still made, mostly in .22 caliber; but the manufacturers also produce rim-fire cartridges in calibers .25 and .41, the latter being intended for the Remington .41 caliber Derringer pistols. Rifles and revolvers used the .32 and .38 caliber rim-fire cartridges in the past, and also the caliber .44, but they are practically obsolete today.

The rim-fire was a big improvement over its predecessors, but it had several faults. The early rim-fire cartridges were subject to accidental explosion when dropped or roughly handled; the crimping of the rim to hold the detonating powder weakened the case so much that a powerful load often tore the base of the cartridge away from the walls with resulting injury to the gun itself; a third defect was the frequency of misfires due to the uneven distribution of the percussion mixture around the rim.

The center-fire cartridge avoided the faults of the rim-fire by using brass instead of copper in the case for increased strength, and by placing the detonating mixture in the center where it was less subject to accidental discharge; by concentrating the priming material in the center, misfires were less frequent.

British authorities credit Charles Lancaster, of London, with the experimental application of the center-fire system, in 1852; but the first center-fire guns made in England used the Schneider cartridge, brought over from Germany in 1861. These early center-fire cartridges had cases composed of a number of parts, one of which was the "anvil," located inside the case, immediately ahead of the primer, placed there to help explode the primer when it was struck by the firing pin or hammer. The manufacturer of this anvil, as well as the other separate parts, kept the cost so high that it discouraged the quantity production of either center-fire cartridges or arms designed for their use.

This problem was solved by Colonel Hiram Berdan, who commanded a regiment of the men who carried the famous Sharps rifles in the Civil War. He devised a plan for stamping the cartridge case out of a solid piece of brass, with the anvil made as part of the shell itself. This reduced costs so much that the center-fire guns and ammunition soon supplanted the rim-fire for all use where powerful loads were needed. Although the Berdan primer was invented and first made in the United States, it was abandoned in favor of a separate anvil more than forty years ago. However, it is still used in the majority of European cartridges.

With this introduction to the story of the cartridge, we can now examine those cartridge guns, both long and short, issued by the United States to its armed forces.

The principal martial *single-shot* rifles of interest to a collector of United States arms are: the Ballard Military Rifle, caliber .54; rifles with Berdan's "slam-bang" alteration (so-called because the breechblock is jointed in the center and makes two clicks when closed suddenly); the Remington-Rider Split-Breech Carbine, caliber .50; the U.S. Rifle, Model 1865, caliber .58, Springfield Rim-Fire; the U.S. Rifle, Model 1866, caliber .50-70, Government Center-Fire; the Ward-Burton experimental Military Rifle, caliber .50-70, Government Center-Fire; the U.S. Rifle, Model 1868, caliber .50-70, Government Center-Fire; the U.S. Rifle, Model 1873, caliber .45-70, Government.

Among the magazine (sometimes called "repeating") rifles and carbines, issued to troops by the United States, the most valuable and interesting is the Colt Model 1855 *Percussion* Revolving Rifles and Carbines. We list them here, among the cartridge pieces, because collectors often ask why the Colt revolving principle was not used more widely on long arms, and why it was not made for cartridges. These arms, made in various calibers, principally caliber .56 for martial use, were not popular with the soldiers, principally because they were not accustomed to revolving arms. These weapons were not well adapted to the use of cartridges because the revolving principle at that time did not permit the construction of a breech strong enough to withstand the backward force of comparatively high-power cartridges.

The regulation magazine, or repeating, United States rifles and carbines ordinarily seen in representative collections are: the Henry Repeating Rifle, caliber .44, Henry Rim-Fire; the Spencer Repeating Rifle and Carbine, calibers .50, .52, and .56, Rim-fire; the Hotchkiss experimental Military and Naval Magazine Rifles, Model 1879, caliber .45-70; the Chaffee-Reece experimental 5-shot Magazine Rifle, caliber .45-70, Government; the Remington-Lee Magazine Rifle, Model 1879, caliber .45-70, Government; the Lee Straight-Pull, U.S. Navy Model 1895, caliber 6 millimeters, U.S.N., rimless; the U.S. Krag-Jorgensen Magazine Rifle, caliber .30; the United States Rifle, Model 1903, caliber .30; and the U.S. Rifle, Model 1917, caliber .30.

All of these repeaters are interesting, both historically and scientifically; but the majority of collectors concentrate on pistols and revolvers, rather than the long arms, which are difficult to store and exhibit; for this reason, we shall proceed to discuss in detail the martial cartridge pistols and revolvers.

There are three United States Martial Breech-Loading, Single-Shot, Cartridge Pistols. These are the Remington Models of 1866, 1867, and 1871. The Colt company did not make any single-shot martial cartridge pistols for issue to the United States troops.

All three of these Remington single-shot pistols were caliber .50; the first, the 1866 Model, used rim-fire cartridges, but the 1867 and 1871 Models used center-fire ammunition.

In arranging a gun collection for display purposes, you can group the arms very much as you please. If you divide the pieces according to their ignition systems, all cartridge guns will be in one group and the percussion weapons in another; but if you separate them according to the loading methods, the repeating rifles will follow the single-shots, and the revolvers will come after the single-shot pistols. We refer to this in the chapter on Classification, and remind you of it here only because it is important to have a clear understanding of types and classes if you wish to build up a significant collection.

In passing from the single-shot cartridge pistols to the cartridge revolvers, we must remember that the percussion revolvers were loaded from the front of the chambers in the cylinder. This is why you will often find the early percussion revolvers listed in museums and dealer catalogues as "front-loading," and the single-shot cartridge pistols described as "breech-loading," thereby distinguishing them from the percussion arms.

Smith & Wesson, as we have already mentioned, made the world's first breech-loading revolver using rim-fire cartridges. This was a .22 caliber revolver, and it is important enough to merit a brief description. On the cylinder of this revolver was marked the patent date, "April 3, 1855"; it was first manufactured in 1856, and it is known that a total of about 58,400 were produced. A specimen now in the possession of the company is marked on the cylinder with patent dates of April 3, 1855; July 5, 1859; and December 18, 1860. Smith & Wesson obtained Rollin White's patent of 1855, thereby obtaining the right to bore the chamber of a revolver clear through. Competing makers thereafter produced arms using fixed ammunition, loaded from the mouth of the chamber, until the expiration of the 1855 patent.

The early Smith & Wesson revolvers are eagerly sought by many collectors, and in spite of the large number manufactured, few specimens are known to be in existence in good condition. This combination of demand and rarity has already made them fairly high priced, considering their comparatively modern origin. Here are the technical details by means of which you can identify the first model; they were given us by Lieutenant Colonel Douglas B. Wesson, Vice President, Smith & Wesson, Inc., and can be considered authoritative:

SERIAL NUMBERS: From "1," up.

FRAME: Brass, nickel plated, round side plate, square butt, sometimes called "silver plated."

BARREL: $3\frac{3}{16}$-inch steel, octagon body with a rib. Blue finish, jointed to top of frame at top strap; stamped on rib: "SMITH & WESSON SPRINGFIELD, MASS." 5 grooves, 5 lands.

HAMMER: Jointed thumb piece to operate cylinder stop on top of frame.

STOCKS: Rosewood or Walnut, not checked. Piano finish.

LENGTH OVER ALL: 7 inches. WEIGHT, 11 ounces.

The first American breech-loading revolver using metallic ammunition, as this term is understood today, was made by Smith & Wesson, operating under patents for both the revolver and the cartridge, on the second floor of a building on Market Street, Springfield, Massachusetts. On the first floor was a livery stable. In demonstrating the mechanism of the first model, the owners once dropped a piece through a crack in the floor and had to search for it in the straw in the stall below. This experience caused them to erect their first building in 1859.

Following the first issue of the first model, Smith & Wesson brought out the second issue, which was first manufactured about 1863. The numbers on the cylinders started in where the first issue left off; hence the first serial number of the second issue was probably 58401. The design was similar to the first issue with these changes: the frame was steel, blue or nickel finish, with an irregular oval side plate; the hammer was made in one piece with a lug on top to operate the cylinder stop by means of a split spring; a few specimens are found with brass frames instead of steel.

In demonstrating the safety of metallic cartridges, Mr. Wesson once hurled one with all his power into a fireplace; unfortunately for the success of the experiment, the edge of the shell struck the sharp corner of an andiron, causing it to fire. "There," remarked Wesson, in a tone of complete satisfaction, "did you note the terrific blow it required?"

The public had been afraid of the new cartridge revolvers at first, but as people became accustomed to handling them, they learned that accidental discharge was usually the result of carelessness. Thousands of the Smith & Wesson first model revolvers were carried as personal, pocket weapons, by officers and soldiers in the Civil War, even though the caliber was too small for official use. Mark Twain even mentioned the new gun in his story of Western life, *Roughing It,* but his remarks were more humorous than complimentary.

With the third issue of the first model, Smith & Wesson started production in 1869, and numbered the revolvers from No. 1 up to No. 128,528. The third issue has the following specifications:

FRAME: Steel, blue or nickel finish, irregular oval side plate, round butt.
BARREL: 3 or 3⅛-inch steel, blue or nickel finish, round body with ribbed top.
CYLINDER: 7 chambers, longitudinal grooves on outside surface.

STOCKS: Rosewood, not checked. Piano finish.
LENGTH OVER ALL: 6½ inches. WEIGHT: 9 ounces.

Shortly after the Smith & Wesson breech-loading revolver came on the market, numerous other manufacturers began to produce revolvers designed for the new metallic cartridges, a good example being the one made by the Rollin White Arms Co., Lowell, Massachusetts. Smith & Wesson brought suit against these companies for infringement of patents, secured judgment, and obtained a court order directing the infringing manufacturers to turn over all finished revolvers and parts to Smith & Wesson. Since many of these weapons were well designed and of excellent workmanship, Smith & Wesson stamped "Manufactured for Smith & Wesson by _____" (naming the company), added the S & W patent dates, and released them for sale.

In addition, Smith & Wesson had contractors who filled their trade orders. For detailed information regarding Smith & Wesson models, variations, descriptions and values, consult the latest revised edition of *The Gun Collector's Handbook of Values.*

Among the many Smith & Wesson weapons liked by collectors, one of the most interesting is the repeating pistol, which used a peculiar cartridge with the fulminate in a hollow at the base of the bullet, and fired this cartridge by means of a sharp projection on the end of a bolt. This pistol, called the "Volcanic," or the "Model 1854," was first made in 1852. It is *not* a cartridge revolver, but it is important as the forerunner of the Winchester repeating rifle action, since the cartridges were loaded by a method which was later incorporated into the Winchester.

The first model .22 caliber rim-fire revolver we have described is only one of several of the early models; other collectors' pieces of importance are the .32 caliber rim-fire of 1861; the world famous .44 caliber Russian of 1870; the .38 Single Action of 1876; the .32 Single Action of 1878; the .32 Double Action of 1880; the .38 Safety of 1887; the .22 caliber Hand Ejector of 1902; and the New Century of 1907. Modern Smith & Wesson models are described in detail in the catalogues of this pioneer company, which is one of the few revolver manufacturers still in business.

Turning to the Colt Revolvers, we find that since the death of the inventor, Samuel Colt, the company has maintained the high ideals of the founder with the help of numerous inventors and mechanics. For several years after the end of the Civil War, the company continued to make percussion, front-loading revolvers, partly to meet the demand of people accustomed to the older type, but principally because Smith & Wesson owned the patents for revolver cylinders in which metallic cartridges could be loaded from the rear, as they still are today. The patents expired about 1873, and Colt's promptly produced their famous "Peacemaker."

The "Peacemaker" was not only the first Colt breech-loading revolver but is also famous as the single-action, center-fire, Army, .45 caliber six-shooter carried by Indian fighters, cowboys, and prospectors. Made in .44 and other calibers, it was called the "Frontier" Colt. Such men as Wild Bill Hickok, Wyatt Earp, Bat Masterson, Luke Short, Neal Brown, and other characters of the wild and woolly West, hung up their old percussion revolvers and made this

Colt cartridge revolver the final arbiter in their personal disputes. Issued to the Army, the Peacemaker was carried through the Indian campaigns in the West and used in battle as late as the Spanish-American War.

In 1877, Colt's introduced their first double-action revolver, made in various calibers and barrel lengths, the Army model being .45 caliber, with a peculiarly shaped grip, called by collectors the "bird's-head model" because, when turned upside down, it resembles the head of a bird. This arm was made for the Army with an ejector for throwing out fired cartridge shells, but the gun never became standard for issue to troops. The Smith & Wesson revolvers were close competitors because of their faster loading method, and they maintained their position until Colt's developed their lateral-swinging cylinder and improved ejector in 1887.

A .38 caliber double-action Colt was adopted by the Army in 1894, using the swing-out cylinder which is still found on modern revolvers. Improved models of this same gun were adopted in 1896, 1901, and 1903, but the soldiers in the Philippine campaign complained bitterly that a .38 caliber bullet was not sufficient to stop a brave and savage enemy like the Moros. There are several authenticated records of Moros who continued to charge our soldiers with their bolo knives until three or four .38 caliber bullets were fired through vital parts of the body. Driven forward by Mohammed's promise that soldiers of his faith who died in battle would be taken at once to Paradise, the Moros would disregard their wounds, close with their enemies, and retain their own lives until they had dispatched their victims. One thing, and one thing only, ever stopped a Moro in his mad rush, and that was a .45 caliber bullet through the brain or heart. The United States learned its lesson and adopted, in 1909, Colt's .45 caliber New Service Revolver; the Marine Corps, motivated by the same sad memories of losses at the hands of the Moros, adopted the same revolver, but with a smaller, rounded stock.

In collecting cartridge revolvers with a martial background, you may acquire specimens of arms made by Bacon, Forehand & Wadsworth, Hopkins & Allen, Merwin & Hulbert, Plant, Pond, Prescott, and Remington; but the two outstanding manufacturers of revolvers in the cartridge period have been Colt and Smith & Wesson.

In 1911, after eleven years of investigation and five years of practical tests, the United States adopted the Colt .45 caliber Automatic Pistol as its regulation side arm for the Army, Navy, Marine Corps, and Coast Guard. It has since gone through several modifications, but it is still known to the regular forces, and to the veterans of the World Wars, as the "Model 1911." In those great conflicts, no finer pistol or revolver was carried than the automatic invented by Browning, and named for that Yankee genius, Samuel Colt.

Collecting automatic pistols is a field of its own. Among the foreign makes you will find the Borchardt, Luger, Bergman, Mauser, Mannlicher, and Browning, the latter being named for the same man who invented the Colt automatics. When automatics were first introduced, our government considered those we have mentioned and also the Roth, Glisenti, Knoble, White-Merrill, Savage, and Shoube. Later, in the early months of World War I, a new pistol, the Grant-Hammond, was submitted to the U.S. Army Ordnance Department for examination; but it was more bulky and clumsy than the Colt, and it was still in the experimental stage, so it was rejected.

We have only mentioned a few of the thousands of makes, models, calibers, and variations of cartridge rifles, revolvers, and pistols. No one can say for sure how many varieties exist in the Colt line alone. Major H. B. C. Pollard, an English writer, said, in his book, *A History of Firearms:* "A representative collection of Colt revolvers can, without being exhaustive, reach to one hundred and twenty-five specimens without having a full range of barrel length and caliber of all types." American experts generally say that if Pollard erred it was on the side of conservatism, that the number of representative types is far greater. A complete text on guns for the collector has never been written; if one ever appears, it will be encyclopedic in scope, with as many big volumes as you will find in the law library of the United States Supreme Court.

The collector is advised to study carefully the Bibliography in this text because references to cartridge arms are scattered through many books, although the author has described in detail and given values for the arms most popular with collectors in *The Gun Collector's Handbook of Values.*

IX

FREAKS AND ODDITIES

ONE OF THE MOST INTERESTING SPECIALTIES IS THE collecting of freaks and oddities, sometimes called combination and special purpose arms. The subject is not as narrow as one might think, for these peculiar firearms have appeared in various forms ever since gunpowder was invented; they are not confined to any one historical period, nation, or manufacturer. They range in age from the primitive hand cannon with a spear on one end to the latest burglar-alarm gun, and in type from ladies' tiny muff pistols to the navy flare, or signal pistols.

Freaks and oddities are popular with collectors, especially with the beginners in our hobby; many of them are exceedingly rare, and yet most of the rarities in this class are within the reach of the man or boy with only a few dollars to spend for guns. This seems like a contradictory statement, for popularity creates demand, and demand usually raises the price. If there is any logical explanation, it lies in the fact that collectors specializing in a particular field of firearms may avoid the freaks and oddities which do not fit into an exhibit. The navy signal pistol, for instance, is correctly classed as a firearm, and therefore it might seem to belong in a collection of "martial" weapons; but its purpose is far from an offensive one; therefore, the specialist in military and naval guns is willing to sell it or

111

trade it for one more closely linked with campaigns and battles.

Collectors of some of the weapons we have included in this classification may feel that their arms are neither freaks nor oddities; they may prefer the more dignified terms, "special purpose" and "combination" guns. Disregarding terminology, we shall discuss in this chapter those firearms which do not logically belong in other parts of the book and which are too interesting to dismiss with a brief definition in the Glossary. There are many ways to group them into classes, but we shall offer them to you in alphabetical order.

ALARM GUNS. An alarm gun in its true sense is one which discharges powder, but no bullets; in other words, it fires a "blank." A typical example is the American Cartridge Alarm Pistol, patented in 1874, which fires a blank, .22 caliber, rimfire cartridge. It consists of a small rectangular steel frame, screwed to a window or door jamb. On one side is a spring-driven arm with a firing pin on its end. This arm is pulled out, and held away from the cartridge by the closed door or window. Opening the door or window releases the pressure, the arm flies forward, hits the cartridge, and explodes the powder charge.

APACHE PISTOL. This is a combination of a revolver, brass or steel knuckles, and a dagger or knife. Many have been made and sold in Belgium and France. It has long been the favorite weapon of the "Apaches" in the slums of Paris.

BAR PISTOL. A bar pistol has two or more chambers cut out of a rectangular, solid metal bar. A typical example is the German Bar Pistol, which has four chambers in the bar, and two barrels. The two cartridges in the top chambers are fired first; then the bar is unlatched and revolved through a complete circle to expose the other two chambers for firing. It was designed this way so that it would lie perfectly flat in the hand or pocket, for concealment.

BATTLE-AX PISTOL. This is a good example of a "combination gun." The butt of the pistol serves as the handle for a battle-ax. Most examples are found in the wheel-lock period, but they are also found in the early flintlock period.

BLUDGEON PISTOL. Here is another firearm with a double purpose. The pistol is designed so that the barrel forms a handle for the club-shaped butt. "Bludgeons" are found in many ignition periods, even as late as the percussion era.

BOOTLEG PISTOL. This type of pistol was usually designed for target practice and dueling, and made to carry inside a bootstrap. A good example is the Gibbs, Tiffany & Co., .34 caliber, rifled, percussion pistol with a 6-inch barrel, made without a trigger guard.

BOX LOCK. In the "box-lock" type, the hammer is inside the lock plate, but projects through between the stock and the lock plate. An example is the N. P. Ames Percussion Box-Lock Navy Pistol, patented 1844.

CANE GUN. Cane guns were formerly made in quantity in France, England, and Belgium for naturalists, game-keepers, and poachers. They are sometimes designed with a concealed trigger, and made so that they can be separated into three parts for ease in carrying, or for hiding in a pocket. Only a close inspection will reveal the presence of the gun inside the cane.

CANNON BARREL PISTOL. The term "cannon barrel" may refer only to the shape of the barrel, but it is also used to refer to pistols, especially some of English manufacture, in which the barrel was unscrewed, the charge loaded from the breech, and the barrel then screwed back into place for firing.

CLOVER LEAF. This refers to the clover-leaf shape of a cylinder, especially the cylinder on the four-chamber Colt House Pistol.

COFFEE MILL. A workman in the government arsenal at St. Louis, during the Civil War, conceived the idea of placing coffee mills in the butts of Sharp's carbines, provided with detachable handles, for issue to the soldiers, one being supplied for each company. Several carbines were so altered.

CUTLASS PISTOL. This term could be used to refer to any pistol with a knife or dagger attached, but it usually refers to

Elgin's Patent Percussion Cutlass Pistol, made by Morrill & Blair. It has a 3-inch barrel, is 12 inches over-all, and it is a .36 caliber, single-shot pistol, with a 7-inch knife blade, 1 inch wide, mounted underneath the barrel, the rear end of the blade serving as a trigger guard. It is believed that less than fifteen specimens are in existence.

DAGGER PISTOL. This is another name for a knife pistol.

DUCK FOOT. A "Duck Foot" is a multibarrel pistol with the barrels radiating from the handle at angles like the fingers of the hand when spread out, or like the toes of a duck's foot. The inventor's intention was probably to provide a weapon that could be fired at several men without changing the position of the shooter's hand.

HARMONICA. The shape gives this piece its name. There are a number of rifled barrels drilled through a solid block. Behind the barrels, an equal number of cartridges, usually pin-fire, are held in a perforated frame. As the trigger is pulled for each shot, the barrels automatically travel across the face of the cartridge frame, the direction of travel being either sideways or up and down, according to whether the barrels are mounted horizontally or vertically.

KNIFE PISTOL. Knife pistols are of two general types. In one, the knife or dagger is merely auxiliary to the pistol; in this form, it is a "combination" gun. In the second type, the knife's chief function is to conceal the presence of the pistol, and it requires a very careful inspection to reveal the presence of the firing mechanism. Sometimes there are two blades, and a few specimens even have a buttonhook and a screw driver with the blades. One of the blades may serve as a trigger.

KNUCKLE-DUSTER. Knuckle-dusters have been made by various manufacturers and in different calibers and sizes, but the most famous model is the "J. Reid, 'My Friend' Knuckle Duster." J. Reid was a gunmaker during the Civil War. "Knuckle-dusters" are also known as "brass knuckles." They are merely a series of holes in a solid metal bar in which a man can insert his fingers so that when he hits another man, he will deliver a hard blow. However, a knuckle-duster pistol or revolver has a large, flat metal butt, with a hole in the center for grasping with the fingers, regardless of whether or not the firearm has been discharged.

LADIES' PISTOLS. This is merely a general term for small-caliber pistols that can be carried in a lady's handbag. "Muff pistols" belong in the same class. They are made in various sizes, shapes, and calibers, and may fire one or more rounds.

PALM PISTOL. A true palm pistol is one made to be concealed in, and fired from, the palm of the hand by squeezing a movable part. One type must be held with the arm extended to the front while the other type is fired with the arm at the side. There were at least three early Pennsylvania gunmakers named "Palm," and there have been men of the same name in recent periods who have made firearms, but the term "Palm Pistol" is seldom confused with their products.

PENCIL PISTOL. This pistol looks like a pencil and is made to fire only one shot. It has a soft rubber knob on the end to act as a cushion in the palm. A ring around the pencil cocks and fires the gun. "Fountain Pen" pistols based on the same general design were made within the last few years to fire gas cartridges, but it is possible also to load them with ball cartridges. When thus loaded, they will fire, but they will do the shooter almost as much harm as the intended victim.

PENNY PISTOL. This is just a toy, made of cast iron. A one-cent piece is placed in a slot behind the hammer; when the trigger is pulled, the penny flies through the air, driven by the blow from the hammer. It is not a firearm, but specimens can be seen in serious collections.

POWDER TESTER. This is an apparatus for testing the strength of gunpowder, sometimes called an *Eprouvette*. There are many forms and sizes of powder testers. The usual type consists of a flintlock mechanism which causes the powder to work against a spring and indicate its strength on a dial.

RING TRIGGER. Revolvers, rifles, and carbines in the percussion period sometimes had "ring triggers" for revolving the cylinders, separate triggers being used for the firing.

SALOON PISTOL. This is another term for "Parlor Pistol," usually a light, small-caliber target pistol; but these names are sometimes applied erroneously to larger pistols and revolvers. The inference, of course, is that they are safe to fire indoors.

SIGNAL PISTOL. Other names meaning the same thing are "Flare," "Parachute," "Rocket," and "Very," the last word being the name of the inventor, Lieutenant Very of the U.S. Navy. A pistol of this type has an extremely large bore; the modern model is loaded with a cartridge which resembles a 12-gage shotgun cartridge. A missile projected into the air ignites and lights up the surrounding area. There is a choice of several colors for the flares, and one kind has a slowly descending parachute.

SHATTUCK "UNIQUE" PISTOL. The "Unique" was well named. It has four .22 caliber, 1⅜-inch barrels bored in a block that tips down to unload. There is no trigger; instead, there is a movable portion of the frame that is squeezed inward to revolve the firing pin and fire each barrel in rotation. The Shattuck is a true palm pistol, but its repeating feature is unusual.

SPRING GUN. This gun was fastened to a tree, or anchored to the ground. Instead of a trigger there is a lever with a hole in it for fastening one end of a string stretched across a path. Anything touching the string moves the lever and fires the gun. Sometimes this is classed as a trap gun.

TINDER LIGHTER. Before friction matches were developed, people had to save glowing coals to start a fire, or use flint and steel. Sometimes the flintlock on an unloaded gun served the purpose, but a more convenient device was the "tinder lighter." This resembles the lock on a flintlock gun, but there is no barrel; instead, there is a metal receptacle for holding tinder (any very inflammable substance) to catch the sparks.

TRAP GUN. Spring guns are sometimes called trap guns, but a typical trap gun is the one patented by F. Reuthe in 1857. It has two .25 caliber, 3¼-inch barrels bored in a block of cast iron. Between the barrels is a spear arrangement that projects from the face of the block. On top of the block there is a heavy spring and trigger mechanism fixed over the nipples. When the spear is pushed back into the block, the hammer falls and fires the gun, the idea being that the spear could be baited to tempt some animal.

TURRET GUN. This gun gets its name from a cylinder closely resembling the cheese-boxlike turret of a battleship. The inventor was John W. Cochran; the most valuable turret revolvers and rifles for collectors were based on his patents and made by the firm of Allen & Cochran. In one type, the turret is vertical; in the other it is horizontal. French-made turret arms are rare but much lower-priced in America than the Allen & Cochran guns. This is also called a "Monitor" because of its resemblance to the Civil War vessel of that name. C. B. Allen, of Springfield, Mass., made a caliber .36, percussion, 7-shot Monitor about 1837.

ZIG-ZAG. This refers to a method of revolving the barrels of a Derringer by means of a stud engaging the angular grooves in the barrels, similar to that used in the modern British Webley-Fosbury automatic revolver; but among collectors the term "zig-zag" is usually associated with the Remington Zig-Zag Derringer, a piece which is extremely rare but comparatively low-priced considering its popularity and rarity.

X

CLASSIFICATION

How to Collect with a Purpose

THE FIRST FEW GUNS YOU ACQUIRE MAY DETERMINE which direction you will travel in this fascinating hobby. A flintlock musket handed down in the family from your ancestor who fought at Bunker Hill may lead you to specialize in Colonial and Revolutionary martial arms, or you may have a cap-and-ball revolver your grandfather carried in the Civil War, and this may influence your choice of percussion arms as your favorite field of collecting. Your decision is a personal one, but it will add to your fun and profit if you collect with a purpose instead of gathering guns in a haphazard manner.

Some collectors specialize in U.S. martial arms, starting with a general assortment, but they usually narrow their field to either hand guns (pistols and revolvers) or shoulder arms, muskets, musketoons, rifles, and carbines), and eventually they often cut down the field of specialization even more. When this happens, they may collect only U.S. martial flintlock pistols, U.S. martial percussion pistols and revolvers, or U.S. martial cartridge pistols and revolvers. In a like manner, they may prefer to specialize in U.S. martial shoulder arms of the flintlock, percussion, or cartridge era. Instead of specializing in U.S. martial weapons, some collectors concentrate on manufacturers' products, such as Colt, Remington, Smith & Wesson, or other makes, but these groups are so broad that they are usually subdivided into groups wherein it is easier to acquire a representative showing.

Classification simply means the systematic division of guns into groups for the purpose of helping you to select, exhibit, or list the pieces in your collection. There are no arbitrary rules for this procedure; you are free to follow your own whims, and even the most advanced collector cannot criticize your choice as long as you have some sort of plan and attempt to follow it. There are, however, some logical principles which apply to any collection, whether you collect guns, stamps, coins, glass, china, or etchings. In this book we limit ourselves to Shoulder Arms and Hand Guns, sometimes called Long Arms and Short Arms, since few gun collectors are interested in cannon or machine guns.

Gun classification does not permit assigning guns to neat, rectangular compartments, fitting accurately together and mutually exclusive, like a printer's type case, into which the collector may drop his guns as a easily as the printer distributes type. The divisions of gun collecting are more like a lot of circles, each having its own fixed center, but overlapping one another at their circumferences.

This is comparable to stamp collecting. Most of us who are active in this hobby started with a small general collection of both foreign and United States stamps consisting mainly of stamps which we bought for a few cents, or obtained in trade for our duplicates. As the collection grew, we found that it was impossible to acquire even a small fraction of the stamps of the world; so we decided to specialize in the issues of a single country, or in those issued in commemoration of some historic event, or those with pictures of birds, or perhaps we chose air-mail adhesives as our field.

We can find another illustration in the field of education. The majority of teachers seem to believe that a broad, general education is the best preparation for life, but there are others who advocate an early choice of a vocation and special training leading toward that goal. There are merits in both contentions; the chief objection to specialization seems to be the difficulty of making an early choice. A similar situation exists in any collecting hobby; all we can do is to examine the possibilities and leave to you the final decision.

You may have a U.S. Flintlock Musket, Model 1795, caliber .69, and want to use this as the starting piece. If you are content merely to gather guns, there is no limit to your next acquisition; but if you wish to collect according to a plan, you have a sufficient number of choices to permit concentration on an interesting and profitable specialty. Your musket is a flintlock; this belongs to an ignition period and you may rule out its predecessor, the wheel lock, and its successors, the percussion and cartridge guns. It is a smoothbore, and hence you may collect nothing but arms without rifled barrels. As a military gun, it is a good start toward an exhibit of military-naval guns, excluding sporting arms; but here you may decide to confine your attention to other long-barreled arms, omitting revolvers and pistols even though they may be military weapons. Your musket is also a muzzle-loader; the later breechloaders may not interest you. If you find that it was used in the War of 1812, here is a historical association that can carry you into a colorful and patriotic specialty—war guns. Thus, we see that classification is neither dull nor arbitrary; it is not a strait jacket, but a signboard in a desert pointing to the fountain of firearm fun.

One of the best classification systems is that used by the Public Museum of the City of Milwaukee, Wisconsin, which owns the Rudolph J. Nunnemacher Collection of Projectile Arms. The Museum's catalogue is divided into two parts: the first includes Long Arms, and the second discusses Short Arms. This separation is purely arbitrary, but it is a convenient method and one widely used by both private collectors and museums, in listing their arms. For exhibition purposes, however, the long arms are placed in racks or high glass cases against the wall, with the short arms of the same class in low glass showcases immediately in front of the corresponding shoulder weapons.

Each of the two parts of the Milwaukee Museum catalogue begins with the earliest type of guns and progresses by periods to the latest type. These periods are not strictly chronological because it is impossible to say that the flintlock period ended and the percussion era began on any certain date; instead, they overlap, as do all the periods in firearm history. The Milwaukee Museum follows the wise practice of listing its weapons primarily according to *Progress in Ignition Methods,* and only secondarily according to progress in loading, rifling, or aiming methods. The reason for this emphasis on ignition progress is that the method for setting fire to the powder charge in the gun has always been the most serious problem of gun designers; this has affected loading, aiming, and rifling systems which could not advance successfully without improvement in ignition.

Neither the Milwaukee Museum nor any other museum will list definite dates for the begining and ending of gun periods because this is impossible. In the first place, the periods overlap. Matchlocks, the most primitive type of gun except the crude hand cannon, are still used in China. Arabs and the Negroes of Africa still carry flintlocks.

A second difficulty in fixing dates is that there is no agreement among arms historians as to which date to select. It is generally admitted that the percussion period was the result of the invention of Forsyth, that Hall made the first American breechloader, and that Colt invented the first commercially successful revolver. Even these statements are disputed by European authorities who claim prior inventions for other men. If we accept the majority opinion, shall we date the percussion period from the day when Forsyth was granted his patent, from the completion of his first model, or from the year when percussion guns came into fairly general use by the public? If the beginnings of the gun periods are in dispute, the endings are still more open to question; in fact, how can we say that they have ended when we find nearly every historical type still in use somewhere on earth today?

We do agree, however, that the hand cannon came first, followed in order by the matchlock, wheel lock, flintlock, percussion, and cartridge periods. This is the recognized order of progress in lighting the powder charge behind the bullet; it is the rational basis for our primary classification of guns.

The ignition method is usually the primary means of

classification, but the loading method comes next. Almost all guns were muzzle-loaders in the early days because there was no known way to prevent the gas from the powder explosion from leaking at the breech. This leakage diminished the power behind the bullet, endangered the shooter, and carried powder ash into the mechanism, where it caused stoppages.

Breech-loading is generally considered as fairly modern, but Lieutenant Colonel Patrick Ferguson of the British Army adopted a flintlock breechloader which may have been carried at the Battle of Brandywine in the American Revolution. His selection was a success, but it was soon forgotten after his death at the Battle of King's Mountain; and this is why we usually date the breech-loading period from the invention of John Hall who perfected a rifle of that type in 1810.

Breechloaders are subdivided, mechanically, as Lever, Bolt, Slide, and Automatic Action. The first gets its name from a lever under the grip which may be used on a single-shot, or with a magazine for extra cartridges with a repeater; the Bolt Action has a bolt that works something like a bolt on a barn door; the handle is pulled up and back to extract and eject the empty cartridge case, and then forward and down to insert a fresh load and lock the mechanism. A Slide, sometimes called a "Trombone," Action, has a sliding forearm; pulled to the rear, it ejects the empties; moved forward, it loads the live rounds into the chamber. Automatic and semi-automatic rifles use either the recoil of the gun, or the gas from a fired cartridge, to work the mechanism which reloads and cocks the rifle.

Pistols and revolvers have their own loading methods. A

pistol may be defined as a short-barreled firearm designed to be aimed and fired from one hand. It is therefore classed as a Hand Gun or Short Arm, whichever phrase happens to please the owner; into this class go single-shot pistols, revolvers, and automatic pistols.

A modern revolver is a small single-barreled firearm with a revolving cylinder containing several cartridges to enable rapid firing without reloading, but this definition would not fit all revolvers which preceded the invention of Samuel Colt. Some early revolvers had several barrels which either rotated or slid (up and down or sideways) in front of the firing mechanism, one of the best examples being the "pepperbox," in which several barrels rotated about a central spindle.

Modern revolvers are divided into two general types. The first is variously called "solid frame," "swing-out," or "side ejection." In this type the cylinder swings out to the left of the solid-framed action. The second is the older "break frame" or "hinged action," with a top strap which is unlatched from the breech, permitting the barrel to swing upward to open the gun for unloading or loading. This is also called a "top break" and a "tip up" type. All four names refer to the same thing.

Older revolvers, such as the Colt Single-Action Army, have a cylinder that can neither be tipped up nor swung out, and there is no extractor. The cartridges are loaded, one at a time, through a loading gate at the side of the frame; and the fired cartridges are shoved out, one at a time, by an ejector rod fastened to the side of the barrel.

In classifying by size, Long Arms, or Shoulder Weapons, is a term which includes muskets, rifles, carbines, blunderbusses, and shotguns. Strictly speaking, the word "Musket" or "Mousquet" refers to a particular type of matchlock, invented about 1540, but the word is commonly used to refer to any long arm with a smooth bore. A "Rifle" is a long arm with its barrel grooved internally with spiral channels to insure greater accuracy of fire, but some of the early rifles had straight instead of spiral grooves; so this definition should omit the word "spiral" to be all inclusive. A carbine is a rifle with a short barrel, intended for the use of mounted soldiers.

Everyone knows what a shotgun is; but few collectors realize that the shotgun is the descendant of the blunder-buss, which was nothing more than a short, muzzle-loading musket with a large bore and a flaring muzzle; loaded with lead balls, broken glass, nails, and stones, it spread destruction in its path at short ranges. Strangely enough, most collectors are disappointed when they first see a blunderbuss; they seem to expect it to have a greater flare or "bell" to the muzzle than actually exists; but this idea is probably based on the fact that the illustrators of our schoolbooks incorrectly portray the Pilgrims going to church armed with funnel-shaped guns.

Hand Guns, or Short Arms, are usually described as Belt Models, Pocket Models, and Saddle, or Holster, Models; these terms are fairly descriptive. Pocket models are usually the smallest, with belt models larger, and saddle models the biggest of all. The large pistols are also called "Horse Pistols" because they were carried in a holster fastened to the saddle.

A "Deringer" may refer to any of the guns made by the Philadelphia gunsmith of that name, from pistols to rifles;

but when the word is spelled "Derringer" (with two r's), it includes all short-barreled pocket pistols of large caliber. Deringer was the originator of the type that took his name, and his guns were extremely popular. To trade on his reputation, competitors brought out similar models which they called "Derringers" to avoid lawsuits. Most people spell the word with two r's in either case, and even the dictionaries show that spelling; but if you want to play fair with the memory of a fine old gunsmith, use only one "r" and forget the dictionary.

Dueling pistols were designed for accurate and reliable fire at a range of 20 to 30 yards; most collectors' specimens are either flintlock or percussion; they often have hair triggers; and they are generally decorated with fine engraving, gold, silver, and ivory inlay, and possess beautiful wooden handles. This is an interesting specialty; and although quite a few good pairs of dueling pistols can be obtained at reasonable prices, a few pieces are beyond the reach of the average collector.

A collection of decorated arms—guns with engraved metal parts, gold and silver inlay, and checkered stocks—is an attractive exhibit; but the best of decoration is usually found only on the finest of guns, since a man who could afford extra workmanship would naturally buy the best gun available in the first place. This is a specialty open only to those with a big budget for gun buying, and one that we do not recommend to the beginner.

Historically, pistols made for formal duels were not inlaid, engraved, or otherwise ornamented because any ornamentation would catch the light and present an excellent target. Since a man's life was at stake, he usually had his dueling pistols made very plain in appearance, but at the same time they were highly accurate, comparing favorably with modern target pistols at the usual dueling range of twenty yards. Since they required expert loading, they were equipped with depth charges, rods, mallets, and other tools, all of the finest material and workmanship. In spite of these facts, collectors often prefer the highly ornamented specimens, which were usually presentation pieces and not true dueling pistols.

We now leave the classification of arms according to their *Mechanical* characteristics and come to that colorful field of *Historical* association, which divides according to Nationality, Gunmakers, Historical Use, and Regional Background.

The great gunmaking nations have been the United States, England, France, Italy, Germany, Spain, and Belgium; each has produced its own military arms, and each has had men who have stamped their names on firearm history with their masterpieces of precision and accuracy. Collectors generally prefer to specialize in arms of their own country, but there are several American hobbyists who have concentrated on the flintlock pistols of such London makers as D. Egg, W. Ketland, and H. Nock; others have favored the Italian flintlocks of Cominazzo, Inzifranci, Lazarino, and Minelli.

Of all the foreign guns, those of English make, particularly flintlocks, are liked best by collectors. Our common heritage of culture and language has something to do with it, of course; but the main reason is that most fine arms, particularly pistols, used in the Colonies before the Revolution were of English manufacture. These were carried by officers and mounted men in the war for independence, thus giving them a historical association which enhances their interest and value.

Second only to English arms in popularity are the rifles, muskets, and pistols of the French which were used by the American forces in the Revolution and then copied when we began to make our own weapons. Third in interest are the rifles of the Swiss, Germans, and Austrians, which, when greatly modified, became the accurate and typically American "Kentucky Rifle."

Next to the early flintlocks with a martial background are the percussion pistols and revolvers of the nineteenth century, especially the Colts. Samuel Colt is the favorite of the collectors, not only because his was the first commercially successful revolver, but also because his career typifies the Yankee genius for invention and salesmanship. By the sheer weight of his perseverance and personality, Colt made the halls of trade and politics ring with his name, until the word "Colt" came to mean "revolver," just as "Stetson" means "hat."

Colt was only one of a long list of gun inventors and manufacturers. More than four hundred gunsmiths are known to have made Kentucky flintlock rifles; at least fifteen hundred men, and a dozen women, from the Colonial days to the present, are recognized by advanced collectors and their weapons included in comprehensive exhibits. There were actually many more; and as historians resurrect old manuscripts from the dusty files, we shall add to the roster of Americans who have contributed their intelligence and dexterity to the cause of national defense and the pleasures of the hunt.

As we add to our collections, we may want to specialize in guns used in battle. An example is the .44 caliber Henry repeating rifle carried by some Indians who participated in the Battle of the Little Big Horn, commonly called "Custer's Massacre." This repeater may have been supplied by agents of the U.S. government in accordance with a policy of helping the "forgotten man." Unfortunately, the soldiers of Custer's Seventh Cavalry were armed with Single-Shot Springfields, lacking the rapid rate of fire of the repeaters in the hands of the Indians. For a reasonable amount you can buy either one of these historic arms, and there is every reason to believe that the gun you buy was actually carried in that memorable engagement.

Guns carried by famous people are another specialty. One collector, for instance, owns the .44-40 single action revolver with a 7½-inch barrel carried by Annie Oakley, the markswoman whose name is perpetuated in the theatrical world as a slang term for free show passes. Another one of his possessions is the caliber .36 Manhattan revolver used by Belle Starr, the "Queen of the Outlaws," when she murdered the sheriff in Dallas, Texas. Pancho Villa's single-action, .45 caliber Colt is still another of the guns linked with the lives of picturesque characters.

Regional arms are in another interesting class. Southerners often specialize in the guns of the Confederacy, such as the Lemat Revolver which was brought from France through the Union blockade, or the Confederate-Colt Navy Revolver which was made in the South during the War; but their favorite pieces are guns designed by their own people and turned out, often by hand, in obscure shops.

In the West, people are proud of their pioneer ancestry

and like to exhibit objects intimately associated with the early days. Even the late-comers, the men and women from the East and the Middle West, collect and treasure what they term "Western" guns, not because any of them were made on the Pacific Coast, but because of the historical connection with the West. One example is the Sharps Buffalo Gun, made in calibers from .40 to .50; another is the Deringer Percussion Pistol, especially when it is stamped with the name of a San Francisco jobber, for then you can be reasonably sure it was carried by a California banker or gambler (sometimes there was no difference) in the "Days of Gold." Still another is the Colt Single-Action Army Revolver, carried by many cowboys, some of whom took their own side arms with them when they followed their hero, Roosevelt the Great, to Cuba with the Roughriders.

We have mentioned the Wells-Fargo messengers' Colt revolver, but there were many express companies in the West, and all of them armed their drivers, guards, and messengers with revolvers, not only Colts, but also other makes; and these guns are sometimes stamped with the name of the company. There is no limit to the number of interesting side trails you can discover when you become a gun collector.

XI

IDENTIFICATION

———————

How to Recognize Valuable Guns

YOU MAY OWN A VALUABLE GUN WITHOUT SUSPECTING its worth unless you understand something about the science of identification. Even dealers who have been in business for many years occasionally fail to recognize a rare gun and sell it for only a fraction of its value. There is an old adage that "knowledge is power" which certainly applies to gun collecting. In this chapter we give you a few simple suggestions which may mean the difference of hundreds of dollars in profit if you stay in the gun-collecting game for any reasonable length of time.

The easiest means of identification is to take your gun to an expert for comparison with one in his collection. If the two guns agree in every detail, recognition is simple; but there may be a variation in the length of the barrels, the caliber, or the shape of the trigger guard. This sometimes happens even when the make and model are the same. Most of the valuable guns are well known to advanced collectors and offer little difficulty; but one made by an obscure gunsmith or a gun which was an experimental model may require reference to old records, catalogues, and books.

Start your identification process by examining the letter-

131

ing on the gun. Thus, the rare and valuable Paterson Colts are all marked "PATENT ARMS. MFG. CO., PATERSON, N.J. COLT'S PT." Collectors would save themselves a great deal of disappointment if they would memorize this lettering and remember that a Colt is not a "Paterson" unless so marked. Gun editors and museums are flooded with mail from people who fondly hope that any old Colt must be a Paterson. If they would pause for a moment to examine the lettering, this would not happen.

There are minor variations, but in general the early Colt models are easily distinguished from each other, by lettering alone. Thus, the Model 1847 is marked "ADDRESS SAM'L COLT, NEW YORK CITY, U.S. 1847"; the Model 1848 Dragoon is marked "ADDRESS SAM'L COLT, NEW YORK CITY, COLT'S PATENT"; the 1848 Pocket Model is marked: "ADDRESS SAM'L COLT, NEW YORK CITY"; and the Model 1849 Pocket Revolver is marked: "ADDRESS COL. SAM'L COLT, NEW YORK, U.S. AMERICA."

Another good example of lettering is that found on the Peabody-Martini Long-Range Creedmore Rifle No. 1. This is not generally classed as a rare or valuable gun, but the lettering is so complete that it gladdens the heart of the beginner who is perplexed by identification. On the barrel this rifle is marked: "MANUFACTURED BY THE PROVIDENCE TOOL CO., PROVIDENCE, R. I., U.S.A.," and also: ".44 Cal. 100 GRS." On the frame it is marked: "Creedmore" and "Peabody and Martini Patents."

The patent dates on guns sometimes confuse collectors. The Colt Army Model 1860 Revolver, for instance, is marked on the cylinder "Pat. Sept. 10, 1850," and you will find this same marking on the Model 1862 Belt and Pocket Models. This patent granted Colt in 1850 covered two improvements in design which he incorporated in the manufacture of all subsequent models; but, for some reason which has never been explained, only the 1860 Army, and the 1862 Belt and Pocket Models were stamped with the patent date. Unless you happen to know that the patent date did not determine the model designation in this case, you might assume that you were examining an 1850 Model, for, as a general rule, the patent date is chosen as the model date.

Agents' names are sometimes found on a gun. Some of the Deringer Percussion Pistols are marked "N. Curry, San Francisco," "F. H. Clark & Co. Memphis, Tenn.," or with the names of other agents on the barrel. This gives little trouble, because you will also find the gun marked "Deringer Philadel," "Deringer Philadela," or "Deringer" with some other spelling of Philadelphia. The difficulty comes when a gun is marked only with the agent's name, or when the same model is made by a succession of owners. This has happened very seldom in arms history, the best example being the "Plant" revolvers, which are found with the Plant name on some specimens, while others are marked "Merwin & Bray," and still others are stamped "Eagle."

When the name of the maker, the name and year of the model, and the caliber are all shown on the gun, identification is fairly complete as far as a beginner is concerned; but an advanced collector may look for signs of military use, such as a stacking swivel or a bayonet lug, or he may measure the length of the barrel; however, these are matters more of classification than identification.

RARE AND VALUABLE PATERSON COLT REVOLVERS

TOP: Paterson Colt Extra Long Barrel, "Texas" Model 1836. 9 inch, scant, octagon barrel, caliber .36, 5 shots, concealed trigger, straight cylinder with two rounded bands, 11/16-inch apart; the bands are formed by narrow grooves running parallel around circumference of cylinder. Between the bands is an engraved scene of a stagecoach holdup, instead of the usual centaurs. This holdup scene is different from those on later Colts. In rectangle marking the beginning and end of the scene is the name "COLT" in Roman type lettering. Round cylinder stops. Rear sight on hammer nose is a separate piece from hammer. Low blade front sight. Front of chambers are chamfered out. Shoulders between nipples are square and not rounded as in some specimens. All numbers are the same, 238.

CENTER: Paterson Colt Revolver, Caliber .28, 5 shots. Walnut grips, concealed trigger, bands similar to above Texas Model; between the bands are centaurs firing revolvers. Round cylinder stops. Barrel marked "Patent Arms M'g Co. Paterson. N. J. Colt's Pt." All numbers same, 132.

BOTTOM: Paterson Colt with Loading Lever. 3-inch octagon barrel, caliber .28, 5 shots; walnut grips. Concealed trigger, round cylinder stops, cylinder engraved with centaur scene. Loading lever and rammer permanently attached to the barrel. Loading lever held in place by hook-shaped spring as in Walker model. All numbers, 385. This is believed to be the last Paterson model made by the original company.

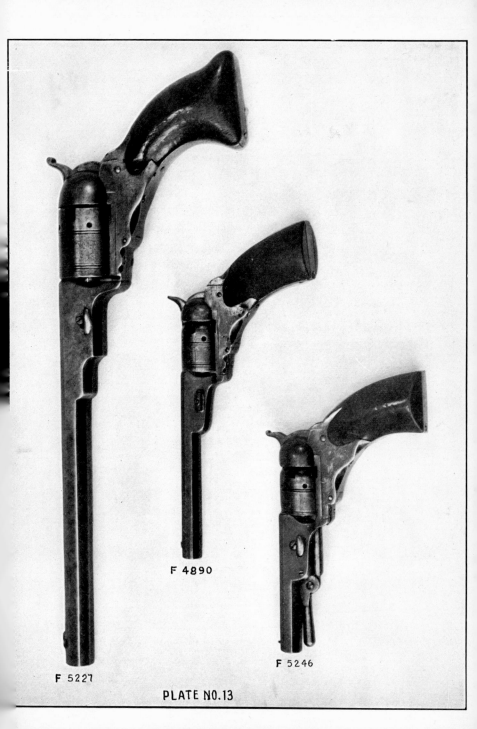

F 5227

F 4890

F 5246

PLATE NO. 13

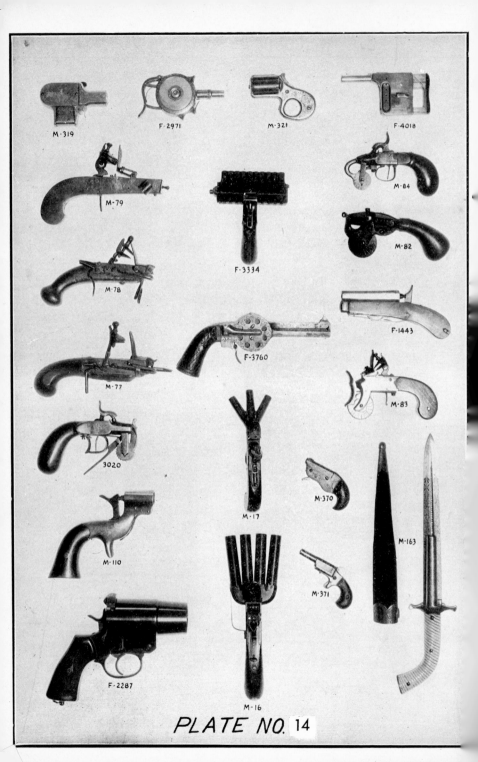

M·319

F·2971

M·321

F·4018

M·79

F·3334

M·84

M·82

M·78

F·3760

F·1443

M·77

M·83

3020

M·17

M·370

M·110

M·163

F·2287

M·16

M·371

PLATE NO. 14

FREAKS AND ODDITIES

LEFT COLUMN:
M-319, C. S. Shattuck "Unique" Pistol
M-79, Flintlock Tinder Lighter
M-78, Flintlock Tinder Lighter
M-77, Flintlock Tinder Lighter
3020, Belgian Eprouvette or Powder Tester
M-110, Civil War, U.S. Army Flare Pistol
F-2287, British Webley World War Signal Pistol

CENTER COLUMN:
F. 2971, Chicago Protector Palm Pistol
M-321, "My Friend" Knuckle-Duster
F-3334, Belgian Harmonica Pistol
F-3760, French Pill-Lock Turret Pistol, Noel system
M-17, English Duck-Foot Flintlock Pistol
M-16, English 4-Barrel Flintlock Pistol
M-370, Hopkins & Allen Pistol
M-371, J. M. Marlin Pistol

RIGHT COLUMN:
F-4018, French "Mitrailleuse" Palm Pistol
M-84, Percussion Powder Tester
M-82, Matchlock Powder Tester
F-1443, Unwin & Rogers English Knife Pistol
M-83, English Flintlock Powder Tester
M-163, French Percussion Double-Barrel Dagger Pistol

Guns of the Colonial and Revolutionary periods of American history present an extremely difficult problem because the makers often omitted their names. The usual reason was that gunmaking was a local business, almost as common as blacksmithing, and the gunsmiths were so well known to their customers that they felt no need for placing their marks on their wares. There were exceptions, of course, in the case of extremely skillful men who were so proud of their guns that they marked them carefully; but even these expert gunsmiths fell into the habit of omitting their names during the Revolution when the British threatened reprisals against any Yankee gunsmiths who were caught supplying arms to their countrymen.

Collectors who specialize in early American arms were fooled for a long time by the letters "CP" found on flintlocks. They thought that these were the initials for "Continental Property" and they were innocently encouraged in their delusion by Charles Winthrop Sawyer, an author of several excellent books on gun history who was accepted as an authority twenty years ago. Sawyer was sincere in his belief, but he was prone to take the word of earlier authorities without always checking their source material.

Today, we know that "CP" did not stand for "Continental Property"; instead, this was the mark of the Commonwealth of Pennsylvania. This fact is a result of studying ancient documents and although historians admit the possibility of this mark being used during the Revolution, the weight of their opinion is on the side of the year 1797 as the earliest date for "CP." The controversy might not seem important were it not for the interest collectors show in arms definitely associated with historical periods.

Next to the lettering on a gun you may find a serial number. This is especially true of guns of the percussion and cartridge types. The U.S. Rifle carried by the armed forces of the United States, for example, always has a serial number which the sailor or soldier memorizes as a means of identification. If a man is a member of a rifle team, he may be issued an exceptionally well-made rifle described as being in "National Match" condition; and one of these rifles has the serial number on both the rifle and the bolt. Likewise, the government model, .45 caliber Colt Automatic Pistol has the same serial number on several parts of each gun. Although these .45 caliber Colt automatics are intended primarily for the federal forces, they are also sold to the general public, including law-enforcement organizations, although most sheriffs and police officers prefer revolvers.

Serial numbers are important to a collector for a number of reasons. First, a low serial number usually indicates that the gun was one of the first guns made in that model or group and hence it is a true representative of that model, untainted by later modifications. This is not always the case, but the rule holds good often enough to justify dealers in asking a higher price for a low number than for a high one.

Second, a gun in the original factory condition, with all or its original parts, can be expected to have uniform numbers throughout, and this increases value since it precludes the probability of some of the parts being modern reproductions. Lack of uniformity, however, does not necessarily lower values when a gun is a recognized "conversion type." This expression refers to guns such as the Colt-Thuers Conversion Army Model 1860, which was a conversion from percussion to cartridge ignition, providing for the use of cartridges instead of the old "cap-and-ball method." This conversion was accomplished by means of a movable steel plate, containing the firing and ejecting mechanism, fitted between the cylinder and the recoil plate of the revolver. Conversions such as this are great favorites with advanced collectors, and they illustrate the wisdom of remembering that there are exceptions to every rule. If we had no exceptions—nothing but iron-clad rules for recognizing and appraising guns—it would take much of the fun from collecting. These little bypaths from the main road provide the variety that makes gun collecting a hobby with an infinite number of possibilities for the gun lover.

A third reason for wanting uniform serial numbers in a gun applies principally to guns using smokeless and semi-smokeless powders. A lack of uniformity in numbers may indicate that the gun was composed of "assembled parts"; they may not fit accurately, with the result that the gun jams just when it is needed; or they may include a part made of poor material that breaks in an emergency. In the pre-cartridge days of black powder, there was little danger of a gun blowing up in the shooter's face; so there is no reason for you to be unduly alarmed about a lack of uniform numbers in an old type. Even if you are selecting a modern gun, this danger factor may not be present if the parts were assembled by a careful and reputable gunsmith.

This discussion of danger in firing might seem out of place to a collector who never intended to shoot his guns; but if you are a red-blooded American there will come a day when you find yourself tempted to take down the old fowling piece from the mantel over the fireplace and fire it, just to see what your ancestors were up against when they needed food, or wanted to repel uninvited boarders.

There is a fourth reason for inspecting serial numbers, and this is probably the most important one of all. By referring to the records of the U.S. government, or to the records of the manufacturers, we can usually fix the historical period during which military arms were manufactured and used. Obviously, it is much easier to say when they were made than when they were used, for in every war we have found a shortage of guns of the latest type, with the result that obsolete guns were pressed into use.

Inspectors' marks are another valuable source of identification. These are technichally known as "Proof Marks," especially when they denote that a gun has been test-fired, but the term "proof mark" in its widest sense includes marks made by inspectors who do not necessarily fire the gun, but merely examine it for mechanical efficiency and conformance with specifications. They are necessary because all fine guns, particularly those made for a government, are inspected many times during their manufacture. Each inspector has his own allotted tests, and a stamp, usually his initial, which he pounds into the metal of the gun part he has found satisfactory.

The practice of proving firearms apparently started in 1637 when a royal charter was granted to the gunmakers' guild of London which authorized them to have the final authority in the testing of all firearms. This London guild later become known as "The Gunmakers' Company," and it still functions with authority to inspect firearms to be sold anywhere in the British Commonwealth, whether or not the guns are made in the Commonwealth. "The Guardians" is a similar organization, with its office in Birmingham, another center of the English arms trade.

If you find the letters "VP" on a gun that has been sold in the British Commonwealth, it means "Viewed and Proved." The first step, called "Viewing," consists of tests to see that all parts have the necessary tolerance, that they are assembled properly, and that the gun functions well mechanically. At the end of this process, the letter "V" is stamped on the gun. Next, heavy charges are fired to see if the gun is safe; if it is, it is regarded as "proved" and the "P" is stamped.

Collectors of early American guns will find that sometimes the letter "P" meant "proved," but it often meant "Provincial" or "Pennsylvania," so here again we must be on guard to avoid against any sweeping generalities.

Unlike Great Britain, the United States does not require the proving of commercial arms before sale; but because American guns are sold widely in countries which do require proving, most arms makers prove all guns intended for export; and some few, notably Winchester and Colt, prove every gun they make, even if it is a low-priced .22 caliber rifle made for sale to boys. Each American gunmaker has his own stamp, and this is also different from the European practice which provides for a uniform system of stamping.

Proof firing, as we have said, means that heavier charges of powder are loaded in the test than the maker expects the ultimate owner to use in actual shooting. This proof firing is of two kinds: Provisional Proof and Definite Proof. Provisional Proof is accomplished while the gun barrels are still in a rough shape, so that unnecessary labor will not be wasted on a barrel unfit for assembly. If the barrel passes this test, a preliminary stamp is placed on its surface. Definite Proof takes place after the whole gun is assembled, and this tests not only the barrel but also the other parts. If satisfactory, the assembled gun is given the Definitive stamp.

With the advent of smokeless powder, sometimes called "nitro" powder, a new set of proof marks were adopted by some of the countries having a uniform proving system; the difference between the two sets of marks thus gives a good indication of age.

Closely connected with the proof marks are marks of government ownership. The British use a broad arrow, and the United States has the phrase "United States Property" on its arms, the latter being of comparatively modern origin.

The British broad arrow started with King George I in 1714 and has continued until the present time. Throughout the reign of the first four Georges, the arms of the British forces were stamped "G.R.," for "George Rex," but this ended with the close of the reign of George IV, in 1830. On some of these guns of the four Georges you will find a crown interlaced with the "G.R.," but the absence of the crown does not invalidate the significance of the "G.R." as an indication of the period.

These government ownership marks are not stamped on a gun until it has been proved. Probably the most famous mark is the word "Tower," which is often found on flint-locks of British origin beside the crown and the "G.R." This word "Tower" is generally believed to indicate that the gun was made for the government; but the correct view is that it is primarily a proof mark, and not restricted to guns owned by the British government. Needless to explain, "Tower" refers to the famous Tower of London, which has been at various times a palace, prison, arsenal, and fort.

European proof marks are controlled by legislation and only given at centrally located testing plants; England, France, Western Germany, Belgium, Spain and Italy have such plants, as does also Austria. The United States has no law on the subject, and no central proof plants for all arms. Instead U.S. government inspectors do most of the proving at the factories, and then only for arms sold to the United States. Each gun factory has its own inspectors, and those which fire proof loads generally employ a powder load which gives about 40 per cent excess pressure, which is sufficient to test the safety factor.

The importance of understanding something about proof marks becomes apparent when you realize that there is a great demand for Colonial and Revolutionary flintlocks, both as collection pieces and as fireplace decorations, and that this demand creates a temptation for unscrupulous dealers to represent arms as "Revolutionary" which were made years after the end of the Revolutionary War. One example is the sale of flintlocks bearing the letters "BGP" and crossed scepters. The crossed scepters do not disprove Revolutionary associations, but by consulting any list of British proof marks we can find that "BGP" was a Birmingham proof mark first used in the year 1813.

Probably the most common swindle is to pass off Belgian flintlocks as something other than Belgian. Belgian guns are chosen because Belgium has produced a great amount of flintlock arms for sale at low prices to natives of undeveloped countries, especially Africa, where flintlocks are still used in hunting and warfare. The center of this trade is the city of Liége, Belgium, which has a big proof house using the letters "ELG" in an oval, with the "E" on one line and the "LG" below.

The "E" stands for "Epreuve," which means "proof." The "LG" stands for "Liége." Below the "ELG" there is usually a star, also within the oval. On top of the oval there may be a crown, or there may be a rough representation of a monument of the city. This monument is an obelisk or tower based on a terraced foundation; but when carelessly stamped on a gun, it looks more like a vertical line with three V-shaped marks underneath.

If you are offered a gun described as a great rarity and of some origin other than Belgian, be sure to look for the proof marks; if you find "ELG" in an oval, with or without the crown or monument symbol on top, you can be sure that the gun is a Belgian piece doctored up to sell to a beginner.

There are many proof marks. Probably the best discussion of them appeared in *The Gun Digest,* an annual publication, which carried articles on proof marks in their issues for 1954 to 1960.

Passing on from proof marks as guides to origin and age, we find that the wood used in the stock of a musket or the handle of a pistol has identifying value. Curly maple was the favorite wood of the best of the early American gunmakers, especially those who lived in the New England states; but other popular American woods in the early days were cherry, red birch, red maple, American black walnut, and dogwood. However, wood in itself is no sure test of origin, for there was nothing except the expense involved which would prohibit a European from importing American wood, or vice versa. An expert on wood can tell at a glance the kind of wood it is, and the regions where it is or was most commonly obtained.

Another clue to identity, which must be handled carefully, is a "hallmark" on silver mounting. Hold a magnifying glass over the silver and you may see the tiny symbols called "hallmarks." If the silver work is English, consult Chaffer's *Book of Hallmarks,* which is available at most large libraries, and you can find the year in which each important hallmark was used. Remember, this only indicates the age of the silver; the gun itself might be much older than the silver mounting. Furthermore, hallmarks are not always found on the silver, and their absence should not be construed as reflecting in any way on the origin or age of the gun.

Caliber means the diameter of the bore of the gun, the inside diameter of the barrel. It is measured between the "lands"—the high places in the bore—not between the grooves, or recessed portions of the bore. Caliber can also mean the diameter of the projectile. In either case, the caliber is expressed in inches for American arms, and in millimeters for European arms. If you find a European gun marked as to caliber in millimeters, as it usually is, multiply the number of millimeters by .03937 and you will have the caliber in inches, which will be the American designation.

Theoretically, this works out all right, but there is a trick to it. For instance, you have a European cartridge for a Browning, or a Webley-Scott pistol, and you know it is known in Europe as a 9 mm. Browning cartridge, the "mm." being the abbreviation used for millimeter. If you multiply .03937 by 9, you obtain as a result the number .35433, which means that the equivalent American cartridge should be a little less than caliber .36. Actually, there is no true U.S. equivalent for the 9 mm. Browning Long or the Webley auto pistol.

The answer is that the Europeans try to list the true caliber, while American manufacturers only approximate the correct caliber designation. You can verify this for yourself by measuring the diameter of the bore of American guns with calipers, and you will find that in many cases the measured caliber does not coincide with that announced by the maker. Thus, the Colt .38 Special Revolver measures .346 inch between the lands and .353 inch between the grooves. The bullet for this revolver has a diameter of only about .359 inch, so the .38 Special Revolver is actually caliber .36.

This is no criticism of American gunmakers; this practice is general and well known among firearms experts, although few laymen realize the situation. This procedure is not intended to exaggerate the size of guns; it works the other way, too. The .38-40, for instance, measures .401 inch between the grooves, and yet it is called a caliber .38 by the manufacturers! Once you understand this, you will know that it is a waste of time to identify a gun by the actual measurement of its caliber; you must refer to the manufacturers' catalogues and learn what caliber they assigned.

Steel was not used much for gun barrels in the United States before about 1846. Iron was the usual material. Since they were muzzle-loaders, there was a certain amount of wear and tear from the ramrods, but this had little wearing effect on the barrels; the real wear came from the friction between the bullet and the barrel on discharge, plus the erosion caused by the hot powder gases resulting from the combustion. Even modern rifles made of the best steel lose their accuracy after a few thousand rounds have been fired; so it is easy to understand how guns made of iron or soft steel were worn away until they required larger bullets than they were designed to fire by the maker. This was naturally true of rifles, which had to be re-rifled several times in the course of a few years of firing. Therefore, when we read that an early American gunsmith made all his rifles in caliber .50, and we then find a rifle marked with his name which measures caliber .60 or even .75, this is no indication that the gun is a fake; it probably means that it had seen hard service and was re-rifled.

Some collectors specialize in shotguns. Instead of caliber, we express their bore diameter as a "Gauge"; this comes down to us from the ancient days when gauge indicated the number of round lead balls of the same diameter as the gun bore which were required to make up one pound in weight. Thus, a 12-gauge or 12-bore gun has a bore of such diameter that 12 pure lead balls of a diameter just to fit the bore would weigh one pound.

"Gauge" is the modern term; "Bore" is the old word for the same thing, although "Bore" also means the inside of the barrel of a rifle, revolver, shotgun, or pistol. Our ancestors were very particular about what words they used in describing their guns; but by looking at the following table of modern shotgun gauges and their equivalents expressed in decimal fractions of an inch (the way we would express their calibers if they were rifles or pistols), we can see that an American patriot who carried a 28-bore musket had a gun with a caliber of .550 inch. The old boys had to have a big bullet to bring down game or enemy soldiers because of their inferior gunpowder; but if we saw a hunter carrying a caliber .55 rifle today, we would know that he was on the trail of nothing smaller than an elephant!

TABLE OF STANDARD DIAMETERS OF SHOT-GUN BORES OF VARIOUS GAUGES

4-gauge .935-inch	16-gauge .662-inch
8-gauge .835-inch	20-gauge .615-inch
10-gauge .775-inch	28-gauge .550-inch
12-gauge .729-inch	.410-gauge .410-inch

NOTE: The .410-gauge is the only one which violates the rule for determining gauges; it is actually a caliber and not a gauge.

We have found that the calibers of guns are listed by the manufacturers according to their own ideas, and not in strict accordance with the usual measurements. This is true for rifles, revolvers, and pistols, but shotguns follow a standard procedure without much variance.

Gun barrels, however, are accurately listed as to length by the makers, but collectors often fail to measure the barrel itself. Since it is attached to the frame, they sometimes take only the visible, outside length, and not the length from muzzle to breech. This is a simple matter and one which should give you little trouble with most arms, but when you attempt to decide on the length of the barrel of a "Pepper-box pistol," trouble begins.

The late Paul B. Jenkins, who was the Arms Adviser to

the Milwaukee Public Museum, took the entire revolving cylinder as the length of the Pepperbox barrel, while other experts have taken the distance from the muzzle to the part called the "nipple." We like the Jenkins method best, because the other way gives a variation as much as ½ inch, depending on which part of the nipple is taken for the end of the barrel.

All of these factors which we have discussed help to arrive at a complete description of a gun. In the absence of comparison pieces in a museum or private collection, your next best step is to compare your description with those found in museum catalogues, dealers' catalogues, and other arms reference material. If this fails, you can then pass your troubles on to the editors of gun departments in the various firearms magazines, or to the curators of museums with firearms collections. If you send them a full description and a sketch or photograph, together with a stamped, addressed envelope, you can reasonably expect a reply fixing the identification of your gun. This is especially true if you own a gun of interest to collectors; it may not be extremely valuable, but if it has historical associations or an important place in the story of firearm progress, you can rest assured that identification will be fairly simple.

XII

HOW SUPPLY AND DEMAND
AFFECT GUN PRICES

ANY HOBBY PAYS DIVIDENDS IN HAPPINESS AND MENTAL
health, and this is especially true of gun collecting with its
wealth of historical and scientific associations. We may be
prone to forget these less tangible returns from our avocation in favor of cash profits; but even then the collector can
have his cake and eat it, too, for well-chosen guns have
been as safe an investment in the last decade as the common
stocks of more than one half of the corporations in the
United States.

Like oil paintings, china, and silverware, fine guns have
no fixed, arbitrary values, and this is one of the reasons why
no standard catalogue of gun prices has been published.
Stamp and coin collectors have their "standard" catalogues,
both in the United States and in Europe; but we must point
out that the prices found in the stamp and coin catalogues
rarely represent the true market value. In proof of this
statement, read any stamp or coin magazine, or visit the
sales rooms of any dealer and you will find that the majority
of all items are offered at discounts below the catalogue
prices, varying from 10% in the case of the rare and highly
desirable specimens to 75% discount for the more common
and less popular varieties.

A stamp dealer, for instance, may attract new business by advertising: "To new customers only, I will sell a collection of 3,000 all different, guaranteed genuine stamps, with a total standard catalogue value of $75, for $5." In view of the fact that catalogue values are for specimens in good condition, we can readily see that, in the case of common stamps, catalogue prices are made extremely high to permit big discounts.

The publishers of stamp catalogues admit this situation, but defend their valuations by pointing out that a dealer with a big overhead may have to charge two to three hundred dollars for the same stamp that a dealer with a small overhead can sell for ten to twenty dollars.

This condition of fictitious values has never existed in gun collecting, but like all collecting hobbies, we find that values are based on three important factors. These are: First, DEMAND; Second, SUPPLY; and Third, CONDITION.

To understand the elements of demand, we must realize that collectors begin to specialize as soon as they have acquired a substantial number of pieces, and their first field of specialization is usually always the objects of their own nation. This is just as true of guns as it is of stamps and coins. Americans prefer American guns, with British arms as a second choice. British collectors choose the guns of their own country first, and then those of America. The result is that British guns command higher prices in London than in New York, and American guns generally bring lower bids in England than in the United States.

A second source of demand is the tendency to collect only the guns of a certain ignition period—matchlock, wheel lock, flintlock, percussion, or cartridge. Just as stamp collectors may prefer the nineteenth century, so many fire-arms enthusiasts specialize in the percussion period which is characteristic of the same century; and this specialization, which is a popular one, enhances the value through demand.

Narrowing down the hobby highway, we find those who not only want American arms of the flintlock or percussion period, but also desire that their specimens be military or naval models; this results in a threefold specialization in national, martial models of a limited period. Revolutionary flintlocks or Civil War percussion guns are typical examples.

A fourth tendency affecting demand is that of preferring short arms to long ones, probably because short arms are easier to exhibit, and more artistic in appearance. A good example of this rule that rifles, carbines, and shotguns are never as much in demand as pistols and revolvers is seen by the sale of Paterson Colt rifles and carbines which are frequently sold at prices varying as low as one-tenth of those obtained for Paterson revolvers and seldom equaling one-half the price of Paterson revolvers, depending upon condition and other factors.

A fifth factor in demand is the collecting of guns made by one man, or by one company. A specialist in American percussion revolvers may favor Colt, while his brother who likes cartridge guns will have nothing but Smith & Wesson models. Likewise, the British flintlock collector may buy only the pistols of Manton, Mortimer, or Egg.

Specialization, then, creates more demand for some guns than for others, and this increased demand raises the prices. We have mentioned here only a few specialties; several more are explained in the chapter on Classification.

Supply, or rarity, is certainly second to demand in its

influence on values. This is best proved by examining the reports on the sales of inventors' gun models. We know of at least one hundred inventors who made only one model, and of several hundred more who made only two or three models of their inventions. If supply, or rarity, were important as a price factor to the collector, these inventors' models would be the highest priced guns, but you can buy them for far less than you would normally pay for better known guns, unless you are competing with a specialist in inventors' models.

Another example of the rule that rarity is not of primary importance is found in the case of shotguns. We have already explained that collectors favor short arms and will pay from two to three times as much for a revolver or pistol as they will for a rifle, carbine, or shotgun of the same make and model. This might seem to be a mere whim or "fashion" in collecting; but when we realize that there are very few Paterson Colt shotguns in proportion to the number of rifles, carbines, and revolvers of the same model, we could expect these shotguns to be extremely costly if rarity were any criterion. Curiously enough, until recently Paterson Colt shotguns were not in great demand but the comments on their rarity in previous editions of *Gun Collecting* have created a great demand and hence they are now valuable items.

At this point, you may well ask how we know what is true about supply and demand in their effect on prices. The answer to this question is that no intelligent and fair appraisal can be made without a thorough study of actual gun sales, and the circumstances surrounding those sales. Sales of guns are made at auction, by dealers, and by private collectors, many of whom are part-time dealers. By obtaining reports on the condition of the guns sold, and the prices they brought, from many sources, over a long period of years, we can not only observe the factors which have established values in the past, but we can also reasonably hazard a guess as to the probable future increases in firearms appraisals.

At first glance, this appears to be a mere job of inventory and simple arithmetic, but the problem is not as simple as it seems. In 1937, for instance, a Paterson Colt revolver sold at auction in New York for $700, while the same make and model, in the same condition, sold for $850 in Chicago, three weeks later. The New York auction was poorly publicized, there was a heavy rain, and the few collectors who did attend were not Colt specialists. On the other hand, the Chicago auction was well advertised, the weather was fair, and there were five Colt specialists present to bid against each other.

Economic conditions have much to do with the prices paid for all art objects and antiques; and although the rise and fall of commodity prices have less effect on fine guns than they do on most collectors' items, we examined the stock and grain market reports for the period between the New York and Chicago auctions we have just mentioned without finding any noticeable fluctuation. This left us right where we started, in the belief that auction sales of guns are not helpful in establishing market values without an investigation into the circumstances surrounding each sale.

Let's take another example to see what happens at auctions. Mr. S, a movie actor whose popularity had fallen off, hired an auctioneer to dispose of his personal effects. Included in his collection of antiques were: a cased pair of Simeon North Flintlock Dueling Pistols, which the actor valued at $600; an Italian Flintlock Pistol by Piero Inzifranci, listed at $500; and a large-type Philadelphia Deringer, listed at $25.

These values were all "reserve prices"; i.e., none were to be sold for less, and this was accomplished by having one of the auctioneer's friends bid for those falling below the "reserve." For this privilege, the actor contracted to pay 20% of the reserve prices for guns offered but not actually sold at the auction.

This auction took place in 1939. The sale was well advertised, but these three guns were the only things of interest to arms collectors. As a result, only one was sold, the Philadelphia Deringer, which was worth about $15, since it was in fine condition with engraved silver plates; but this brought $53 on a sale to a woman who was a "movie fan" and thought that anything owned by the actor was "precious." The other two guns, which were splendid pieces, fit for any museum, were priced at least 35% above their true value, but in the report of the auction they were listed at their reserve appraisals. This auction was typical of 1939 auctions, but today people know more about gun values and auctions more truly represent real values, all of which, of course, are higher today.

If auction reports are deceptive, what can we say about the reports of sales by private collectors and part-time dealers? Sellers like to boast about the high prices obtained, and buyers enjoy telling their friends about a purchase far below the fair price, with little attention being paid to the run-of-the-mine sales that reflect true conditions. For reasons of taxation, few of the advanced collectors talk about their expenditures, preferring to let the tax assessor write their prized possessions down as a "miscellaneous assortment of obsolete guns." For these reasons, we must look further for an honest estimate of market values.

The third, and most timely, of all sources of information, is found in the catalogues published by professional dealers in firearms for collectors. These catalogues may vary for guns of the same make, model, caliber, and condition; but on the whole they come close to the true retail market value because the bulk of their business is done by mail, and this eliminates fluctuations on account of attendance, local economic flurries, and "freak" sales such as the gun sold to the movie fan.

When *Gun Collecting* was first published in 1939, thousands of collectors wrote to the author for advice about the values of firearms they either owned or wanted to buy. Those who gave detailed information about the condition of their arms and described them fully were mailed estimates of value based upon the current market demand and the condition as described by the owners of the guns. They were told that the values quoted were what the guns were worth to a private collector, and that dealers would not pay more than 50% of the retail price, on an average. For low-priced arms, dealers might pay only 25% of value; and for the higher-priced arms they might pay 80% of retail if they knew they could be quickly sold.

At the request of readers of *Gun Collecting,* the author wrote the first edition of *The Gun Collector's Handbook of Values* which was published in 1940. Revised editions were published in 1947, 1951, 1955, 1958, and late in 1960.

Each edition was based upon the advice of many collectors, dealers and museum curators, and reflected their research in the fields of values, condition, identification, and historical association. It is doubtful that any other book for hobbyists has been so thoroughly revised by so many experts over such a long period of years, hence we must of necessity refer to it in this text to guide those who want to successfully organize gun collections of significance.

XIII

CONDITION

————————⌁————————

And How It Affects Values

Condition is important, not only in arriving at a correct estimate of the value of your guns, but also for the purpose of describing any duplicates you offer for sale or trade to brother collectors or dealers, and for an intelligent interpretation of the descriptions sent you by others. Coin and stamp collectors have long recognized the need for a uniform method of describing their pieces, and their systems for accomplishing this purpose are fairly standardized; but among gun collectors there has been no agreement in the past.

Stamp collectors first list stamps as used or unused, and then go into such details as whether or not the stamp is "well centered" on the paper, lightly or heavily canceled, and so forth. Coin collectors are more definite in their terminology. To them, "Proof" means that a coin was specially struck for collectors at the mint and has a mirror-like surface. "Uncirculated" means it is like new and has never been used as currency. "Very Fine" describes a coin which has been circulated but shows no signs of wear. "Very Good" means that it is somewhat worn but still a desirable exhibition piece. "Good" means that the type is clear, even though the coin is worn. When it is considerably worn and the type is not clear, it is called "Fair."

Gun collectors have tried unsuccessfully to apply the condition descriptions of coin collecting to firearms; but there is little comparison between the two hobbies, and this forces us to adopt our own expressions. "Proof," for instance, might be applied to fine guns turned out by a factory for gifts to kings, presidents, and generals. Samuel Colt made many such gifts, but those still in existence show the marks of time and wear; so we are content to call them "Presentation Pieces" and put them in a condition class by themselves. In a like manner, we might call guns which were inventors' models "Uncirculated," but the lack of general interest in these models has discouraged any such classification.

Dealers and collectors who buy and sell guns as a sideline realize the need for accurate description and try to meet this need by defining their own condition terms at the head of their trade list or catalogue.

The author has offered various systems of condition classification to gun collectors, and has found that any description which is too strict is unpopular with those who are trying to sell guns although it is very well liked by the buyers. The classification system used in the recent revisions of *The Gun Collector's Handbook of Values* and generally followed by collectors and dealers is as follows:

FINE: At least 50% of the original factory finish. Markings distinct. All parts original. Perfect working order. The amount of the original finish should be given.

GOOD: Little or no original factory finish. Markings absent or indistinct. Barrel may be rusted or pitted slightly. Stock may be scratched, bruised or cracked but sound and complete.

Shows wear but no abuse. Good working order. The amount of rusting and pitting should be carefully stated.

FAIR: No finish on parts. Barrel rusted or pitted slightly, or shows signs of cleaning. Markings absent. Fair working order. Shows much use. Stock scratched, bruised, cracked or repaired. Major parts must be original, but minor parts may be replacements.

The author also recommends that in describing guns, or examining them to appraise their value, you should note the following details which directly affect not only the value of the gun but also its identification and classification:

1. All marks on the gun (lettering, numbers, and pictures).
2. Kind of lock (match, wheel, flint, percussion, or cartridge); rim-fire or center-fire; any indications of alterations to the lock.
3. Number of shots and the caliber.
4. Length over-all.
5. Length of barrel and cylinder.
6. Kind of barrel (round, octagonal, or ½ octagonal); is it rifled or smoothbore?
7. Kind of trigger guard (square, oval, or sheath), and if with or without spur, made of iron or brass.
8. Kind of grip, shape, and of what material.
9. Of what material is the frame made, iron or brass?
10. With or without ramrod?
11. Condition according to *The Gun Collector's Handbook of Values;* note particularly whether the barrel was blued or nickeled, and the extent of the original finish.
12. Of what kind of wood is the stock made?

In the case of military-naval shoulder arms the collector will want to look for a stacking swivel, sling swivels, and bayonet lugs, although all of these are absent from some military-naval models. To the above list, some authorities would add the following items:

Under Number 2, in describing a revolver, or a revolving-cylinder rifle, carbine, or shotgun, describe the cylinder as (a) Straight, (b) Fluted, or (c) Rebated. In addition to the description of the trigger guard, describe the trigger as single or double, standard or set, open or concealed. In addition to the over-all length, in No. 4 of the above outline, give the weight in pounds and ounces; if the gun is a shoulder weapon, give weight with and without the bayonet and the sling.

With this approach to the subject of the effect of condition on valuation, we can now turn to the catalogues of gun dealers and examine the application of our theories in practice. For this purpose we have selected the Colt Pocket Model 1849 Percussion Revolver, caliber .31, made for both 5 and 6 shots, and marked "ADDRESS COL. SAM'L COLT, NEW YORK, U.S. AMERICA," on the model made in Hartford, Connecticut, from 1849 to 1873. The same model, made in London, England, from 1853 to 1857, is marked "ADDRESS COL. COLT, LONDON." The standard barrel is sometimes considered to be the 4-inch barrel, but we have seen this model with barrel lengths of 3, 4, 5 and 6 inches. The standard 4-inch barrel results in a weight of 24 ounces for this revolver; each added inch of barrel length is supposed to add 2 ounces to the weight of the gun.

This Colt Pocket Model 1849 was chosen as an illustration because it is popular with both beginners and experts, is generally stocked by dealers in antique arms, and is available in a variety of prices based on condition. Omitting models in "Factory New" condition, we find this notation in the catalogue of a dealer:

COLT'S POCKET MODEL 1849................$150
4″ octagon barrel, .31 cal., 5 shots, silver plated guard and
straps. All numbers same. VERY FINE with nearly all the
original finish. SCARCE CONDITION.

Notice that the dealer describes his gun as being in "very
fine" condition. He apparently did this because he is con-
scientious and did not want to say that the gun was in
"factory new" condition when it was lacking part of the
original finish. He thus contributes "very fine" as a description of a condition which he regards as intermediate between
our "fine" and "factory new" classifications.

If you are looking for a Colt Pocket Model 1849 to
round out a collection, you may not want to pay quite as
much as $150. If you are willing to pay a little less and
accept one in "good" condition, this excerpt from the same
catalogue will interest you:

COLT'S POCKET MODEL 1849................$100
4″ octagon barrel, .31 cal., 5 shots. Walnut grips. Silver plated
guard and straps. All numbers same. Back strap engraved
"John Young from J. U. Gillespie 1861." Bright. GOOD.

If this price is still too high, a further search will find
that the same gun, without any engraving, is listed thus:

COLT'S POCKET MODEL 1849................$75
4″ octagon barrel, .31 cal., 5 shots. Walnut grip. Silver
plated guard and straps. ABOUT GOOD.

The above are merely examples from the catalogue of a
dealer in antique arms. The prices given are not necessarily
average values for any particular year, although they were
taken from a 1960 catalogue, principally to show how con-

dition affects value. The phrase "ABOUT GOOD" may mean in reality "FAIR," but it possibly means "POOR" condition. Some dealers would sell the same items for smaller prices.

We have thus run the condition range from "fine" to "poor," inclusive, to show you practical applications of condition classification to price; but a word of warning is in order at this point—very few dealers will stock a gun in any condition less than "fair," and it is extremely inadvisable for a collector to buy, or acquire by trade, any gun that is not at least "fair." Instead, you should make every effort, consistent with the state of your gun budget, to buy only arms in "fine" condition. We shall now return to the top of the price list and observe the result of acquiring guns that are not only in fine condition, but are well engraved, stocked with rare woods, and in cases.

Using the same Colt's Pocket Model 1849 as our unit of comparison, and the same dealer's catalogue, we find that he quotes one in good condition, but with "all metal parts engraved," at $250, thus adding $100 for the engraving. The same gun, in a plush-lined, mahogany case, complete with its original Colt's flask with spread eagle and crossed pistols over a ribbon bearing the words "E Pluribus Unum," a brass mold marked "Colt's Patent," a nipple wrench, and a screw driver, would be priced at $400, thereby adding $150 for the original case and accessories. Plain ivory grips would increase the value at least $30; carved ivory grips would add $60 to $90 to the appraisal, depending on the quality and extent of the carving.

We have mentioned that the Pocket Model was made with both 5- and 6-shot cylinders, and that the barrels were made in different lengths. These, too, have a bearing on price, and so does the marking, for some collectors desire only the London model.

Very few Colt percussion arms in "factory new" condition are on the market. The value, without engraving, ivory grips, or accessories, is approximately doubled when sold in the original case, with all accessories, ivory grips, and in fine condition throughout. Again, we must emphasize that the prices quoted above did not represent average prices for 1960, but merely what one dealer expected to get.

Guns which have seen hard military or naval service are seldom found in fine condition. The Colt Model 1848 Dragoon Percussion Revolver is a good example. This model is in great demand by collectors for its historical background. Since demand is more important than condition, they are glad to buy a Dragoon regardless of its condition. Realizing that the comparative condition, rather than the strict terms of the above system, applies to this model, dealers often list its condition as "fine for a Dragoon," or "good for a Dragoon."

Guns which are not in great demand, and hence are quoted at low prices, should not be bought by a collector in any condition less than "good"; but some experts do not agree with this statement and take the position that a gun in any condition, if bought at a proper price, is better than none when it is needed to fill in a gap in a series of representative types or models. If you are collecting with no thought of resale, you may agree with this view.

Another apparent exception to the application of the above classification occurs when a weapon is acquired as a "decorator"—that is, to be hung over a fireplace or on the wall of a den. Since it will not be subject to close inspection, the general appearance is more important than the details of mechanical perfection, but even then it should be selected to harmonize with the historical period of the room in which it is to be displayed. Nothing is more incongruous than a cartridge-model rifle on the mantel of a fireplace of "colonial" design.

In 1934, a grizzled old miner walked into a California gun shop, placed an 1849 Pocket Model Colt on the counter, and asked what it was worth. The dealer examined the gun and saw that it was .31 caliber, with a 6-inch barrel, and in fine condition, but that the grips were made of oak instead of the usual walnut, and that the back strap was engraved with the name of Wm. R. Litchfield, while the words "Charter Oak Stock" were finely engraved on the trigger-guard strap. The dealer sensed that there was something unusual about the gun and asked the owner where he had found it.

"Got it out of an old trunk up in the attic," he explained. "My father brought it with him when he came across the plains to California along with the rest of the gold seekers. I want to sell it. I'm past seventy, going on eighty, and might as well have the money as that old shootin' iron."

The dealer estimated the retail value to be about $30, made an offer accordingly, and the transaction was closed; but all day the words "Charter Oak Stock" kept repeating themselves, over and over again in the dealer's mind. That night he consulted *Armsmear,* a rare book on Colt and his guns, published in 1866 by Henry Barnard. Thumbing through the pages, he found several chapters devoted to the story of Samuel Colt's absorbing interest in the historic

Charter Oak of Connecticut, and an explanation of why the old man's revolver was marked as it was.

The story carries us back to the night of October 31, 1687, when the Royal Governor, Edmond Andros, came to Hartford with soldiers to confiscate the colonial charter of Connecticut and thus deprive the people of the liberties they had enjoyed under its provisions. Just as Andros reached for the charter, the candles were extinguished, Captain Joseph Wadsworth picked up the charter and ran with it to an oak tree where he hid it in the hollow trunk.

The tree, which was known as the "Charter Oak," was blown down during a wind storm on August 21, 1856. Mr. I. W. Stuart, who owned the land on which it stood, gave his friend, Samuel Colt, several pieces of the tree as souvenirs. Colt, in spite of all his mechanical and advertising ability, was sentimental about the tree, for he had played around it as a small boy; so he used some of the wood to make the handles for revolvers which he presented to his friends. Thus the revolver bought from the old man was linked to one of the most colorful incidents in American history.

What was the gun worth? The question can never be answered. The dealer sold it for $75; three weeks later he was offered $100 for the same gun. To a man who is not interested in arms, the iron and wood in the revolver might be worth only its junk value of about four cents; but to those who love guns with an interesting story, its value cannot be measured in dollars and cents. In 1960, the same revolver was worth up to $500.

The majority of firearms for collectors are sold through the mail and shipped by express. Most dealers are honest but there are enough crooked collectors and dealers to make it necessary to issue a warning. Unless the buyer and seller have had mutually satisfactory experiences before, the safest procedure is to ship by express, charges and payment collect, subject to examination and refusal. The buyer can then open the package in the presence of the express employees, see for himself what he is getting, and then either pay or refuse the package and send it back to the owner.

In theory, the U.S. Post Office Inspectors are supposed to investigate cases of frauds conducted through the mails in any manner, whether by false advertising, false correspondence, or by shipment, but in practice they often take no action whatever. Therefore, the author of this text now has goods sent by express, subject to examination, as explained above.

XIV

MAKING A PROFIT
FROM GUNS

———————

$\mathbf{M}$ANY GUN COLLECTORS EVENTUALLY BECOME DEALERS, even if their sales are limited to a small circle of acquaintances. There are at least four reasons for this. First, duplicates are bound to accumulate, especially when you have an opportunity to buy an entire collection at distress prices from the heirs to an estate. Second, if you have some pieces in good condition, you may wish to dispose of them to make room for the same models in fine condition. Third, if you started a collection of U.S. martial arms, including both rifles and revolvers, you may decide to discontinue the long arms and concentrate on the short ones. This is a natural thing to do; for as you learn more about guns, you become interested in some specialty that is narrower in scope than your first choice. Fourth, as your friends discover your knowledge of guns, they will come to you seeking advice on arms collecting; being in a position to render them a real service, you are entirely justified in charging a reasonable commission for the guns that you obtain for them.

What profit may I expect to make from guns? This is a fair question, and the answer is an obvious one. Like any other business, dealing in guns requires knowledge, hard work, honesty, a knack for salesmanship, and a certain amount of what some folks call luck. We know of dealers who have cleared more than ten thousand dollars profit even in a depression year, but they were working full time and understood guns thoroughly. A professional man who started as a collector a few years ago sent two sons and a daughter through college on the profits made from dealing in guns at night and on Saturday afternoons. A few full-time antique arms dealers make an annual net profit ranging from $25,000 to $50,000 per year, but they each employ at least one helper to clean and renovate guns, they have capital to buy collections, they read gun books and magazines, and they advertise extensively.

There is no single substitute for experience in any business, but no one should try to become a dealer until he has read the authoritative books on the various specialties and examined enough arms to distinguish the valuable models from those that are similar in appearance but lacking in the details that make them desirable to the collector. By obtaining the current catalogues and price lists from other dealers, you can strike a rough average for prices; but if these catalogues and price lists do not describe the condition of the pieces offered, or if the dealers are careless in their use of adjectives, their quotations should be given little weight.

Variations in descriptions of condition may be due to plain ignorance; but the principal cause is the lack of any standard, generally accepted system for rating condition, as we explained in an earlier chapter. If you become a gun dealer and solicit trade by mail, by all means preface every list you send out with a frank, clearly worded explanation of what you mean by "Factory Condition," "Excellent," "Fine," "Good," or any other terms you use.

Wise dealers promise "money refunded upon return of the guns if not found satisfactory," and they keep their promise, even when it may have meant the loss of a sale in the meantime to another collector. Most of them do this because they are inherently honest, but the rest do it because they know that no one can stay long in any kind of occupation if he has a reputation for not keeping his word.

You may make a reasonable profit as a part-time, local arms dealer, but the bulk of the guns sold in America is sold by mail. To obtain mail-order business, you must advertise in one way or another. Advertising takes various forms. Probably the best of all may be classed as "publicity"; this is the advertising that costs you nothing. You may obtain publicity by talking on guns over the radio, holding an open-house gun exhibition for the public, or by sending short articles and photographs to the editors of the magazines carrying articles on gun collecting.

Your gun articles may not be literary; but if they are technically accurate and interesting to collectors in general, the editors are glad to revise them to fit their standards of style. You may think: "What'll I write about? Everything has already been said on the subject!"; and if you do, just glance at any magazine or newspaper feature section and you will find that the same old stories are told year after year; the authors merely give them new names and tell them from a new angle. You can do the same with your gun articles, but if you try hard enough, you are certain to discover phases of the gun hobby which have never been discussed in print; and these fresh, vital topics will be welcomed not only by the editors but also by thousands of collectors who will eventually become your customers.

Obviously, you cannot expect to get everything for nothing. Magazines will not continue to "plug" you and your business indefinitely when they learn that you are a dealer and are using the editorial pages as a substitute for paid advertising, but the patronage you receive from the free publicity will usually justify the expenditure of a few dollars per month in the advertising columns.

We have mentioned photographs as a good publicity medium. This is true because every magazine and newspaper in the country welcomes good, clear photographs that can be used as illustrations. The old favorite size was four-by-five inches, but the modern, improved films permit the taking of smaller pictures which can be enlarged if necessary. Size, though, is not the only consideration; the pictures must bring out not only the general appearance of the gun but also the details if it is to interest the collectors.

Magazines with hobby departments are not your only avenue for publicity through photographs. Your local newspaper, and the papers in the near-by cities, will welcome photographs of you and your guns if you can tie in your collection with a "timely" news story. For instance, on "Old Settlers' Day," merchants will beg you to let them display your arms in their windows, and the reporters will run colorful stories about guns used by the pioneers.

The Rotary, Kiwanis, Lions, and other "service" clubs are always looking for speakers. Take along some of your favorite guns, tell the story back of them, and you will not only hold old friends but make new ones for your hobby and your business. Do not disregard the youngsters, either; they may not be customers in the near future, but they go home and tell their parents about the fun to be had from collecting firearms.

When you become known as a collector, whether you are a dealer or not, you will receive countless letters, telephone calls, and personal visits from people who own a "rare old gun that must be worth a lot of money." It will require a great deal of patience and diplomacy to explain that neither rarity nor age necessarily determine value, that many guns more than a century old, and well known as rarities, are worth less than fifty dollars apiece, even in excellent condition. It will take still more tact on your part to avoid offending them if you undertake to point out that the mere fact that a gun was carried by a deceased ancestor does not add to its worth as a collector's piece.

People who know little about guns may write and say: "I have an old Colt six-shooter; how much is it worth?" If they enclose a stamped envelope, the courteous thing to do is to write back and ask them for a detailed description, preferably with a sketch or a snapshot. If you receive many inquiries of this nature, much time can be saved by preparing a mimeographed questionnaire based on our system of classification and condition description. Send this to those who fail to give identifying details in their first letter. If they are really interested, they will fill it out and return it. Out of a hundred inquiries, fifty may be idle curiosity seekers, and forty may be people with guns of little value, but from the other ten you may obtain desirable specimens at reasonable prices. This distribution of percentages probably represents the experience of the majority of the collectors and dealers in America; the favorable returns from the ten per cent justify all the trouble you spend on the other ninety.

"How much should I pay for guns?" Here is another question frequently asked by collectors who are buying arms for their own exhibits, or for resale or trade to others. In this book we have explained in great detail the factors influencing values—demand, supply, condition; these three determine not only what you can hope to charge for the guns, but to a certain extent they also affect the prices you should pay.

For a gun in great demand, you may know of a dozen men who stand ready and willing to take it off your hands as soon as you place it on the market. A Paterson Colt, for instance, is always salable at a good price. The person offering it for sale to you usually knows this, and you may have to pay an amount which gives you only a 10% margin of profit; but your capital is only tied up for a short time, and this 10% may mean as much as $200 profit.

On the other hand, when buying a Deringer, you must remember that there are many Deringers on the market and your money may be tied up for several months. Therefore, you should not pay more than 50% of the price you hope to receive. This 50% profit is probably a good rough average; and it is the experience of business men in general, not merely gun dealers, that 50% gross profit is the smallest profit which can cover such expenses as rent, light, heat, salaries, depreciation, and interest. Out of the 50%, you may lose enough in overhead to cut your actual profit down to 20% or even 10%. This is a rule of thumb if you maintain a shop; if you handle guns only as a sideline to some other business you may be able to afford a smaller profit.

Those of you who are simon-pure collectors may think,

when you read these comments on profits for dealers: "That
settles it; I shall buy all my guns from the part-time dealers
and save money!" That idea holds good sometimes; but,
strangely enough, the big gun dealers can often offer the
more common guns for prices far lower than those asked
by the small dealers. The reason for this is that the big
dealers advertise extensively, are well known to the collectors, and often employ "scouts" who spend their time
looking for collections that are for sale in their entirety.

When a collection is offered for sale, the dealer, or the
collector who merely wants to add to his own collection,
examines the whole lot for the presence of the desirable
pieces; and his offer for the whole lot is fundamentally based
on the value to him of those few guns he wants. This is not
so true in the case of a specialized collection (that is, one
with a reasonably complete representation from all the
types and models in the specialty), but when a collection
is merely an indiscriminately gathered number of guns,
those pieces which have no important place in the exhibit
are not given much weight in arriving at the purchase price.

These extra, "wildcat," guns are then offered for sale by
the collector or dealer for what they will bring, in order to
leave room for the desirable items and to provide capital
for further additions. There may be nothing the matter with
these left-over guns; a dealer may want to get rid of them
because he knows of no immediate market, or the collector
may not be interested in these makes or models. Whatever
the motive for disposing of them, these remnants from collections afford a collector an opportunity to pick up "bar-
gains."

There is another cause for "bargain prices." A dealer

may have a thousand dollars tied up in some special group of guns which for some reason or other do not "move." They will be sold in time, but an opportunity comes to buy two or three valuable pieces which the dealer knows he can sell at a profit immediately. To get the money for the more profitable investment, he can afford to cut the prices of the slow-moving lot to his actual costs; or he may even take a small loss if the profit to be realized from the new guns will justify this action. Consequently, the slow-movers are listed at prices which bring prompt orders from collectors and other dealers.

It may seem strange, but dealers buy from dealers in the gun trade more than they do in almost any other occupation. There is no formally organized guild, but they have mutual respect for one another; and most of them are well acquainted with each other, not only by correspondence, but also through personal visits, for gun dealers are great travelers, always welcoming an excuse to visit collectors and other dealers. A friend or relative may tend the shop while they are gone, and the money spent in traveling is repaid in profits from new pieces added to their displays. This is the only practical example we have ever heard of that exemplifies that old adage about the people who "make their living by taking in one another's washing."

Just as it is often more advantageous to buy from a regular dealer, so it is frequently more profitable to sell to a dealer than to a private collector. If you have only a small circle of acquaintances who are gun collectors, none of them may happen to be interested in the particular gun you offer for sale; or they may lack enough money to pay a fair price. On the other hand, the dealer is in touch with thousands of collectors who constantly send him their "want lists"; and many of these people are willing and able to pay what your gun is worth. Being sure of a quick sale, the dealer can afford to make a small profit on your gun; and he may pay you a price considerably above the usual market value of your weapon.

Most dealers buy for cash, but there are a few who take guns on consignment and act as brokers. To handle this class of trade, they mail out lists of guns sent them by the owners, together with the prices the owners hope to get. From the first mailing they receive checks and money orders from buyers; the commission, usually from 10% to 25%, is deducted, and the balance sent to the owners, with a suggestion as to the next lower prices they may be able to obtain from mailing out a second list. If the owners agree, another list is mailed to prospects, and sometimes a third, or even a fourth, mailing is necessary to close out the consignments.

Collectors who are anxious to obtain certain guns buy from the first list; but if they take a chance on losing an opportunity to fill out their collection by waiting for the lower prices on the subsequent lists, they may be able to buy what they want at a lower quotation. For the seller who is not in a hurry to liquidate, this method offers an attractive and often profitable means of disposing of duplicates.

Dealers co-operate with one another and with collectors in giving information on current trends in collecting, the identification of unusual arms, and valuations; but there is one thing they keep secret, and that is the list of addresses of their customers. A dealer's customer list is one of his most valuable assets; but there is an additional reason, aside from the commercial one, for keeping secret the names of collectors and dealers. This is the fact that many of the advanced collectors do not want publicity.

No one knows for sure why some collectors shun publicity. There are probably several reasons. One is that any news about the great value of a collection will bring a flock of tax assessors to the front door. Another reason is that there are thousands of curiosity seekers who will write, telephone, and personally visit collectors at all hours of the day and night, once they know that they have an interesting exhibit. This applies to all collectors, and it is not strange to find that gun collectors are not alone in their avoidance of publicity; their brother hobbyists in the fields of stamps and coins are equally shy.

Because of this tendency toward secrecy, many gun collectors' clubs are never known to the newspapers or the general public; and the exact number of active, advanced collectors is unknown. Editors of gun columns in magazines estimate an approximate total of 300,000 gun collectors who are constantly buying, selling, or trading guns. The number of those who are not actively in the market, but who buy and read gun magazines and books is even greater.

"What guns offer the best chance for a future increase in value?" This is a question that it is impossible to answer with anything more than a reasonably intelligent guess. At this time the more desirable pieces, those selling for $100 or more, seem to offer the safest investment for the man who wants a steady, upward climb in value. They have increased in value throughout the years of economic trouble without any serious drops; and, since condition and demand are important, they can be expected to increase, rather than decrease, in value.

On the other hand, there are many rarities selling for prices below thirty dollars. The collector or dealer who can "outguess the market," can, by making a wise choice, invest in these lower-priced guns and reap a handsome profit when and if they attract the attention of collectors and a demand for these present "sleepers" forces the market upward. We have mentioned throughout this book many guns in the various price classes.

Specifically, pistols and revolvers are usually a safer investment than rifles, muskets, carbines, or shotguns, the only exceptions to this rule being Kentucky Flintlock Rifles, the early martial flintlocks, and the revolving rifles. Among the small arms, flintlock and early percussion pistols and revolvers are favored more than the late percussion or cartridge types, but a general rule is dangerous. Each gun should be judged on its own merits. Even if you guess wrong, your money is safer in guns than in stocks and bonds.

XV

THE CARE AND CLEANING
OF GUNS

"**I**S IT LOADED?" THIS IS THE FIRST QUESTION THAT A COL-lector should ask himself in examining a gun. The exact procedure for answering this question varies with the various types of firearms, the most difficult being the muzzle-loading muskets, rifles, and shotguns. One method is to run a rod down the bore, mark the distance on the rod, and then compare this distance with the distance from the muzzle to the breech plug. If you are exact in your measurements and there is a difference between the two of approximately one-half inch or more, the gun is probably loaded. Another method is to remove the barrel from the stock and then unscrew the breech plug with a heavy monkey wrench. If the breech plug is rusted to the barrel, soak the connection with kerosense for several days before you attempt to sep-arate them or you may twist the tang from the plug. If all else fails, you may even fire the gun; but this should be the last resort.

Pistols and revolvers are easier to inspect for loads; but it is well to be sure that all barrels, or all chambers in a cylinder, are empty. In the case of percussion arms, look at the nipples; they may reveal the presence of corroded caps, or even the remains of fired caps; these in turn may indicate that the gun is loaded. Even when there is no powder in the bore, primers are a source of danger. Some people have the mistaken idea that when the powder and priming are over fifty years old they have lost their strength; this might be good in theory, but in practice Civil War relics have been known to fire their original loads ninety-five years after they were stored away in attics.

Our ancestors, in muzzle-loading days, were often confronted with the problem of removing the charge in a gun. For this purpose they used a "worm"—a twisted metal rod or wire affixed to one end of a ramrod; this was inserted in the bore and gently revolved until the screwlike worm entered the lead bullet sufficiently to hold its grip when the ramrod was pulled out. Needless to say, they took good care to remove the priming powder from the vent and the priming pan before they started; but even after the bullet was extracted, they had to use the worm again to loosen the packed powder sufficiently for it to fall out of its own weight when the gun was held with the muzzle down. The whole process was a lot of work, and it is not surprising to learn that many men left their guns loaded from one day's firing to the next, or else shot them into the air.

The custom of unloading a gun by firing it must be an old one, for Shakespeare, in his *Merry Wives of Windsor,* tells us that Sir John Falstaff, on one of his romantic expeditions, was looking for a place to hide. He wanted to seek refuge in the chimney, but Mrs. Ford and Mistress Page informed him that he would have to find another place, that their husbands were accustomed to unloading their fowling pieces after a day's hunting by firing them up the chimney.

After unloading the gun, or otherwise making sure that it is empty, you may want to look at the bore, but collectors usually pay little attention to the condition of the bore unless the gun is a modern piece or they want to shoot it. You may be surprised to know that shooting has anything to do with gun collecting, but there is a national organization of muzzle-load collectors with local chapters in a number of cities and towns, and a regular schedule of matches with trophies and prizes awarded to the winners.

To clean the bore, you can use a bronze-bristle brush fastened to a steel cleaning rod, and a bottle of powder solvent. The former can be bought from any hardware or sporting-goods store; the latter can be purchased at the same place, or you can make your own. One of the best home-mixed powder solvents contains equal parts of acetone, pure sperm oil, and the best grade of turpentine. There is nothing mysterious about preparing it except that it is best to put the turpentine in the bottle first, add the sperm oil, and then pour in the acetone last. However, instead of using a solvent, plenty of hot water and soap is regarded as the best bore cleaner by most gun experts.

Work the soapy water or solvent back and forth several times with the brush, wipe the barrel clean and dry with Canton flannel patches, cut about one inch square, using a regular ramrod. Follow this step with the application of a good grade of gun oil on another patch; or, if you have no intention of firing the gun, use gun grease. Be sure that all of the solvent is removed before you grease or oil the barrel, because solvent dissolves grease and oil, and exposes the metal to rust.

Having satisfied yourself that the gun is not loaded, and

that the bore is clean enough to meet your requirements, the next step is to examine the lock. On a flintlock Kentucky Rifle, there are "lock screws" on both sides; remove these first and the lock comes off easily. On other types of guns the names and the number of screws are different, but a little observation will disclose the method of procedure. When the lock is removed, the next move is to compress the main spring; gunsmiths have a special tool for this, but you can do it in a vise. Tighten the vise until the hammer is free from the action of the spring, press down the sear spring, lower the hammer, and you can then lift the main spring from the lock. Continue to strip the lock, laying the parts on your bench in the order in which they are removed.

When the lock is completely stripped, soak the parts in kerosene to loosen the rust, and then follow this with an application of steel wool. When the rust is all removed, oil the parts and reassemble the lock, putting the parts back in the reverse of the order in which they were removed.

Few flintlocks found in storage have flints in good condition. Any piece of flint will not do. Buy your flint from a dealer in antique arms who imports his flints from England where they are "knapped" (dressed down to correct size and shape) by men who do nothing else. Screw the flint between the jaws of the cock with the flat side uppermost. To give the jaws a good grip on the flint, insert pieces of leather which have been soaked with tallow to make them pliable.

If your gun is of the percussion type, you may find that the nipples are badly rusted, worn, bent, or missing. These may be replaced. Remove the old nipples with a special nipple wrench which you can obtain from almost any dealer in gunsmithing supplies; if you do not use the regular nipple wrench, you may break a nipple in the process and then find that it is difficult to remove the broken part left in the cylinder. Nipples have threads, varying from 18 to 14 threads to the inch; there is also considerable variation in their size and shape, so you will want to obtain the correct nipples for your gun, either from a dealer or from a discarded gun of the same make and model. There is nothing unethical about providing an old gun with new nipples, but we shall have something to say later on about how far you can go with gun restoration without being guilty of "faking."

If your lock is now in shape, you will want to turn your attention to the other metal parts, such as the barrel, trigger, trigger guard, butt plate, fore-end tip, and patch box, the number and names of these parts depending, of course, on the type of gun. Brass parts, if the gun is very old, may have a "patina"; this is a dark green film formed by oxidation, and it is one of the reliable indications of age, for it is hard to counterfeit. This should not be removed. Likewise, any browning or bluing on the surface of the steel parts should be left intact if it is the original finish. Original condition is always preferable to a bright steel surface; very few guns were sold "bright"; most of them were browned or blued, the principal exceptions being a few all-steel pistols, or nickel-plated arms. Even in the latter case, it is better to leave the gun as you find it than to attempt to renickel.

Brass or bronze parts may not have acquired a patina; instead, they may be covered with bright green spots that add nothing to the appearance. Wash with a chemical powder copper cleaner, which will remove the copper oxide, but not hurt the metal surface. Then polish with any brass or silver polish.

The outside of the barrel and the other steel or iron parts may have deep rust pits. These are little holes worn in the metal by the action of the elements; there is nothing you can do to remove holes in metal. By all means do not use a wire brush, or emery paper; instead, take out the rust with the finest grade of steel wool, rubbing the steel wool into the pits with your hand. It may require hours to finish the job, but it is worth while. If you use a buffing machine, you may save time, but you will inevitably destroy some of the original surface surrounding the pits.

When your metal parts are free from rust and corrosion, you will want to preserve them from further deterioration. You can do this by coating them with a light film of shellac, lacquer, or ordinary light gun oil for exhibition purposes. For storage, use gun grease. There are a number of antirust preparations on the market which may be better than ordinary oil and grease; you will find them advertised in any magazine catering to sportsmen, and on sale at hardware and gun shops. There is a considerable difference of opinion among experts as to the best antirust preservative. If you examine your guns frequently, you can decide for yourself which one is suited to your conditions.

If you put your guns in storage, build little racks for them in boxes. Do not put them in leather holsters, wrap them in cloth, or put them in contact with paper or pasteboard. All these substances absorb moisture and encourage rusting. Men who use rifles every day find that they rust less when suspended by their slings, or by cords, than they do when they are in scabbards.

The wooden parts of a gun require less attention than the metal parts. Very little cleaning is usually necessary. Rubbing with a rag soaked in linseed oil will remove the surface dirt; but if this fails, rub the surface lightly with the finest grade of steel wool, working with the grain in the wood. When the wood is clean, you can polish it with wax. Never use varnish, this is the worst possible finish for any gun stock.

If the original finish is missing from the stock and you want to take out dents, do not remove the wood from the gun but place a cloth wrung out in boiling hot water on the surface and press it with a very hot iron; the resulting steam will raise the dented portions. If the wood then comes up above the rest of the surface, you will have to level it off with fine sandpaper. In any event, leave the surface of the wood alone if twenty-five per cent or more of the original finish is present.

A previous owner may have ruined the appearance of the wood with varnish. If this has happened, rub the stock with varnish remover on a rag, waiting twenty to thirty minutes between applications. Two applications are usually sufficient to loosen the varnish which is then scraped off with a putty knife. When all the varnish is off, rinse off the varnish remover with water and benzine, let the wood dry slowly, and then finish the stock with several coats of linseed oil rubbed in by hand. There is no use to hurry; there are no short cuts in refinishing wood.

Now we come to a delicate but important subject—the restoration of guns. There are gunsmith's books which explain in great detail how to "restore" old guns. They tell you how to rerifle the barrels, reblue and rebrown the metal, and refinish the wood. They even include instructions for making new ramrods and stocks. All that might not be so bad, but they also go on and give you formulas for supplying the brass parts with an artificial patina, and "aging" the wood.

Why is this information found in books? The answer is that there is a lucrative trade in what we might politely term the "restoration" of arms. It is quite legitimate to add a new trigger guard or a new nipple; but when this is done, the owner should keep a record of the replacements and pass it on to any subsequent purchaser. In Europe, the arms dealers can provide a customer with a record of the ownership of a valuable gun, going back for years—often for a century or more. This practice has not yet become the custom in the United States.

When restoration goes beyond the replacement of a few simple parts, it approaches "faking," outright dishonesty— "cheating" if you want a good old-fashioned word for it. We first warned collectors about faking in the 1939 edition of *Gun Collecting;* repeated it more strongly in the 1947 edition; and regret to report that by 1960 the counterfeiting of the more desirable and valuable arms became a full-time occupation for several men. Let the buyer beware!

However, there is a bright side to the picture. Dealers who advertise in magazines with gun departments are carefully investigated; at the slightest suspicion of fraud on their part—or even the too-frequent commission of "mistakes," they are asked to withdraw their patronage. This does not mean, however, that the absence of a dealer's advertising from a magazine stamps him as dishonest; for some of them have built up a following which absorbs all their offerings, and these men may not advertise at all for months at a time.

If a discussion of fraudulent practice has any tendency to frighten you away from the gun hobby, please remember that anything of value in this world is imitated. Every object bought and sold by collectors is subject to the same blight—stamps, coins, etchings, paintings, silver, pewter, glass, china, furniture—there is not a single exception. The old story about factories with equipment for artificially putting worm holes in chairs is no joke.

"How can a beginner protect himself against deception?" The best advice is to study all you can about guns, visit museums and private exhibits to learn the "feel" of the pieces that interest you, and then, when you are ready to buy guns, trade only with a man known to be both capable and honest. He must be both, for honesty in itself is a poor protection against an intelligent crook.

All of the outstanding, ethical dealers in firearms for collectors regularly stock books on guns, and these same dealers feature *The Gun Collector's Handbook of Values* in their price lists and catalogues. They are not afraid that the collector will learn values. There are a few honest dealers who do not stock gun books but they are comparatively small operators. Those who want more information about home gunsmithing will find it in the author's book, *Gun Care and Repair—A Manual of Gunsmithing*.

XVI

GUN PHOTOGRAPHY

━━━━━━⌇⌇━━━━━━

ONE OF THE JOYS OF COLLECTING IS THE PRIDE OF possession you feel when you exhibit fine guns to your friends. This human and entirely commendable trait is given a new impetus when you exchange photographs of guns with collectors in distant cities. All of us cannot own the same rarities at the same time; but we can do the next best thing by collecting photographs of guns, especially when they are large, clear prints showing the little details of mechanism and decoration that give a gun individuality.

Another advantage of gun photography is that you can send pictures of pieces you cannot readily identify to other collectors, dealers, museum curators, and firearm editors. The Chinese have said that "one picture is worth a thousand words"; this is especially true in the case of arms, for no matter how carefully we may describe or sketch a gun, there is no substitute for a faithful photographic reproduction. Not only for identification purposes, but also for the trade or sale of arms, collectors and dealers are finding that photographs reduce the amount of correspondence needed to inform one another of their offerings.

Most people own some sort of a camera, and although we may not be experts, a little experimentation with lighting and exposure will often bring excellent results from even the most inexpensive equipment. The old-fashioned box camera will produce pictures that give a *fair* idea of the general appearance of a gun if properly handled; but for *good* results use a medium-priced folding camera with a portrait attachment; this attachment costs only a few dollars and enables you to place the camera as close as two feet from the gun.

The late Dr. Paul B. Jenkins, arms expert of the Milwaukee Public Museum, advised everyone who wrote to him regarding the identification of firearms to submit a photograph. For the collector who was not well versed in photography, he offered the following suggestions:

"First, have an absolutely blank, dead-white background. Paper will do, but a freshly ironed sheet is better if it is tacked smooth with no wrinkles. Second, take as large a photograph as possible to obtain strong, sharp lines. Third, get a sharp, brilliant illuminated view."

In taking his own gun photographs, Dr. Jenkins had a table built with a huge sheet of semi-opaque glass for the top. The gun was laid on this glass, and the camera was suspended over the gun. Overhead light came from a 1,000-watt bulb. Under the table were electric bulbs in series so that they could be turned on or off as more or less light was needed. By using the glass between the bulbs and the gun, the light from below was diffused, and all shadows were eliminated. As a result, Dr. Jenkins obtained photographs so clear that small marks on the gun could be examined from the photograph with a microscope almost as well as from the gun itself.

In his day, Dr. Jenkins was outstanding, but the late Dr. S. Traner Buck, of Philadelphia, who was for many years one of the outstanding gun collectors in the United

States, improved upon the Jenkins technique, and although there have been many recent improvements in photography, the Buck method is still highly regarded by collectors.

Dr. Buck also used a glass-top table, but his had three layers of glass. The middle one was opal glass while the upper and lower layers were plate glass. Between the opal glass and the bottom layer of plate glass, he ran a series of parallel lines, one inch apart, so that in the photograph they would appear as a "grid" to enable the collector examining the picture to see at a glance the measurements of the various parts of the gun. These cross lines were formed by using either black thread or very fine black wire stretched on a removable frame, so that the grid lines would not appear if he took out the frame for photographing objects against a plain background.

The object of the opal glass in the Buck technique is the same as the semi-opaque glass used in the Jenkins method —to diffuse the light coming from under the table. As an additional precaution, Dr. Buck covered all the outside wooden surface of the table with white cardboard so that no light would be absorbed by the wood. Under the table were ten, either 40- or 50-watt, frosted incandescent bulbs, arranged in two series, with switches so they could be turned on or off, to obtain even lighting. For direct overhead illumination, two wooden frames were mounted at the sides of the table, carrying ten frosted incandescent bulbs on each frame. At the ends of the table were upright stands holding what the photographers call "No. 1 Photoflood Lamps." Obviously, all of the lights were arranged so that no one series carried too much of a load. Dr. Buck used

40-, 50-, and even 100-watt incandescent bulbs, according to the amount of illumination he found necessary; and he advised the beginner to experiment until he finds the arrangement which best fits his own needs.

Before considering the photographic equipment used by Dr. Buck, let us consider the three general requirements for any camera taking pictures of guns, so that we can use these requirements as a standard by which to test any equipment we may acquire. First, the camera should have a focusing back so that you can see the image in the ground glass for accurately focusing on the object; and it should use either cut film or plateholders for reasons of convenience and economy. Second, it should have a well-corrected anastigmat lens. Third, it should be fitted to a shutter through which time exposures can be made.

If your only hobby is gun collecting, these details of photography may bore you; but there are so many camera-minded people these days, including schoolboys, that you should have no trouble in finding someone who will be glad to take gun photographs for you. However, no matter how good a photographer he may be, the man who has not given special study to close work will need the information furnished here.

Dr. Buck used a 5 x 7, heavy duty, view camera, equipped with a Graflex focal plane shutter. He successfully used three lenses, a Zeiss Tessar f. 4.5; a Cooke 8¼ inch, series II with a Graflex shutter; and a Wollensack 90-degree, wide-angled lens with a Compur shutter, the latter being used usually for time exposures. Other types of cameras can be employed, even a Minicam with the portrait attachment for close work; this is an attachment which is slipped on the lens, and then taken off for distant work. One of the best cameras for all-around photography, which also works especially well in photographing guns, is the Speed Graphic, preferably the latest 2¼ x 3¼ miniature Speed Graphic.

The camera is carried vertically over the illuminated table by an iron bracket. This bracket projects out from the wall of the dark room about three feet. It is made from three pieces of 2½ x ¼-inch, flat iron, welded into a right angle. The front end is turned down; the back is drilled to fit a vertical piece of a shafting-bearing hanger, bolted to the studding in the wall. The bent-down front end is attached to a short board by means of a carriage bolt with a wing nut for locking. On this board slides another board, carrying the camera, which can be slid up and down. The fittings, to permit the movement of these parts, are made from flat, square, and U-shaped brass. The purpose of this apparatus is easily and quickly to move the camera into position over the gun.

The equipment, with the exception of the camera, can all be assembled by anyone handy with tools at comparatively little cost. The cost of the camera is a matter of personal choice. You can make the illuminated table, and a frame to fit a ten- or twelve-dollar camera; the results will be infinitely better than you could obtain with an expensive camera and an improperly lighted object. Not only guns, but also stamps, coins, books, chinaware, silverware, etchings, and paintings can be photographed with this apparatus. There is no limit, except the size of the table, to what you can photograph; if the object is longer than the table, photograph it in sections and then join the sections together.

We have mentioned both cut film and plateholders. Cut film is preferred because it is not only handy and economical but also unbreakable. In buying cut film, ask for a fine-grain film, such as "fine-grain panatomic-x." (The dealer will then know exactly what you want.) With this, you will use a yellow K-2 filter.

In adjusting your lights, have the illumination even both above and below, and experiment with various stops and exposures. For detail, such as fine engraving on a gun, use an "f.18 stop." For a great depth of focus, which occurs when you are trying to show clearly the mechanism of a gun, you may use what photographers call a "42-stop." Then, in printing your pictures, be sure that the developers and paper are chosen for the purpose you have in mind. Glossy paper, for instance, is best to bring out the contrast and detail in gun parts; this is obtainable in five grades according to the amount of contrast you desire.

If you are not especially adept at photography, do not feel any embarrassment about showing this chapter to someone who is; he may be as unfamiliar with the language of guns as you may be with the technique of his hobby. That is one of the sources of fun in gun collecting; when properly pursued, there is no avocation which can bring you so many interesting contacts with people in other walks of life.

Some gun collectors try to maintain a file of photographs of guns and they also like to have copies of illustrations from old and rare gun books that they can borrow but cannot afford to own. The equipment and methods of gun photography described in this chapter have stood the test of time, but the photography of arms and the copying of pictures are constantly being improved. We recommend that you consult a professional photographer, a dealer in photographic equipment, or a successful amateur gun photographer before you invest heavily in this interesting but highly technical phase of gun collecting.

APPENDIX

GUN MUSEUMS

Gun Museums in the United States of America

ARIZONA: Museum of the Old West, Seligman.

ARKANSAS: Saunders Memorial Museum, Berryville.

CALIFORNIA: Disneyland, Anaheim; Los Angeles County Museum, Exposition Park, Los Angeles; M. H. de Young Memorial Museum, Golden Gate Park, San Francisco; Wells Fargo Bank, 22 Montgomery St. at Market St., San Francisco.

COLORADO: Colorado State Historical Museum, 14th Ave. at Sherman St., Denver; Fort Garland, Fort Garland.

CONNECTICUT: The Connecticut Historical Society, 1 Elizabeth St., Hartford; State Library, Hartford; Wadsworth Atheneum, 25 Atheneum Sq., N., Hartford; Winchester Museum, Olin Mathieson Chemical Corp., 275 Winchester Ave., New Haven.

DISTRICT OF COLUMBIA: National Rifle Association of America, NRA Headquarters Building, 1230 16th St., N.W., Washington; United States National Museum, Smithsonian Institution, Washington.

GEORGIA: Chickamauga-Chattanooga National Military Park, Fort Oglethorpe.

ILLINOIS: Chicago Historical Society, North Ave. at Clark St., Chicago; George F. Harding Museum, 4853 Lake Park Ave., Chicago.

LOUISIANA: Louisiana Historical Association, 929 Camp St., New Orleans; Louisiana State Museum, The Cabildo, Jackson Sq., New Orleans.

MARYLAND: Fort McHenry National Monument and Historical Shrine, Baltimore.

MASSACHUSETTS: First Corps Cadets Armory, 105 Arlington St., Boston; Essex Institute, 132 Essex St., Salem; Springfield

Armory Museum, Springfield; Old Sturbridge Village, Sturbridge; John Woodman Higgins Armory, 100 Barber Ave., Worcester.

MICHIGAN: Henry Ford Museum, Airport Dr. and Oakwood Blvd., Dearborn.

MISSOURI: City Art Museum, Forest Park, St. Louis; Missouri Historical Society, Jefferson Memorial Bldg., Forest Park, St. Louis.

NEVADA: Harold's Club, Reno.

NEW JERSEY: Morristown National Historical Park, Washington St., Morristown.

NEW YORK: Washingington's Headquarters, Newburgh; New York Historical Society, 170 Central Park West, New York; The Metropolitan Museum of Art, Fifth Ave. at 82nd St., New York; Fort Ticonderoga Museum, Fort Ticonderoga; West Point Museum, United States Military Academy, West Point.

OHIO: Cleveland Museum of Art, East Blvd. Wade Park, Cleveland.

OKLAHOMA: J. M. Davis Collection, Mason Hotel, Claremore; Fort Sill Artillery Museum, Fort Sill.

PENNSYLVANIA: Bucks County Historical Society, Pine and Ashland Sts., Doylestown; Pennsylvania State Museum, Capitol Hill, Harrisburg; Pennsylvania Farm Museum, Landis Valley, Lancaster; Historical Society of Western Pennsylvania, 4338 Bigelow Blvd., Pittsburgh.

SOUTH CAROLINA: Confederate Museum, Market and Meeting Sts., Charleston.

TEXAS: Texas Memorial Museum, San Jacinto Blvd. at 24th St., Austin; Panhandle-Plains Historical Museum, Canyon; The Carl Metzger Gun Collection Room, Memorial Student Center, College Station; The Alamo, Alamo Plaza, San Antonio; Witte Museum, 3801 Broadway, San Antonia; San Jacinto Battlefield Museum, State Rt. 134, 22 miles southeast of Houston.

VIRGINIA: Fredericksburg National Military Park, Fredericksburg; Marine Corps Museum, Quantico; Virginia Historical Society, "Battle Abbey," 428 North Blvd., Richmond; Confederate Museum, 12th and Clay Sts., Richmond; Colonial Williamsburg, Williamsburg.

WEST VIRGINIA: Huntington Galleries, Huntington.

WISCONSIN: Lincoln-Tallman Museum, 440 N. Jackson St., Janesville; Wisconsin State Historical Society, 816 State St., Madison; Milwaukee Public Museum, Wisconsin Ave. between 8th and 9th Sts., Milwaukee.

Gun Museums in Canada

CANADA: Old Fort Henry, Kingston, Ontario; Royal Ontario Museum, 100 Queen's Park, Toronto, Ontario.

Gun Museums in Europe

AUSTRIA: Steiermarkisches Landeszeughaus (Styrian District Armory), Graz; Heeresgeschichtliches Museum (Army Historical Museum), Vienna; Kunsthistorisches Museum (Museum of Art History), Vienna.

BELGIUM: Musée Royal de l'Armée (Royal Army Museum), Brussels; Musée d'Armes (Armes Museum), Liège.

DENMARK: Tojhusmuseet (Arsenal Museum), Copenhagen.

FRANCE: Musée de l'Armée (Army Museum), Paris.

ENGLAND: H. M. Tower of London, London; Imperial War Museum, London; Victoria & Albert Museum, London; The Wallace Collection, London; The Rotunda, Woolwich.

SCOTLAND: Scottish United Services Museum, Edinburgh; Kelvingrove Art Gallery, Glasgow.

ITALY: Armeria Reale (Royal Armory), Turin.

NORWAY: Haermuseet (Army Museum), Oslo.

SPAIN: Museo del Ejército (Museum of the Army), Madrid; Armería Real (Royal Armory), Madrid.

SWEDEN: Skokloster Castle; Kungliga Armemuseum (Royal Army Museum), Stockholm; Kungliga Livrustkammaren (Royal Armory), Stockholm.

SWITZERLAND: Bernisches Historisches Museum (Bern Historical Museum), Bern; Musée d'Art et d'Histoire (Museum of Art and History), Geneva; Seughaus Solothurn (Solothurn Armory), Solothurn; Schweizerisches Landesmuseum (Swiss Museum), Zurich.

CLUBS FOR THE COLLECTOR

NATIONAL MUZZLE-LOADING RIFLE ASSOCIATION, 12 E. Franklin St., Shelbyville, Indiana. Publishes *Muzzle Blasts*, a monthly magazine devoted largely to gun collectors and muzzle-loading matches. Conducts matches on the Walter Cline Rifle Range, at Friendship, Indiana, and organizes many local and mail matches, especially for those who fire muzzle-loaders.

NATIONAL RIFLE ASSOCIATION OF AMERICA, 1600 Rhode Island Avenue, N.W., Washington 6, D.C. This is a nonprofit organization supported by the membership fees. Its purposes are to educate and train citizens of good repute in the safe and efficient handling of firearms; to foster a knowledge of small arms and the ability to use them among members of law enforcement agencies and the armed services, and all other citizens who would be subject to service in the event of war; to promote social welfare and public safety, law and order, and the national defense. Membership in the N.R.A. is available to any reputable citizen of the United States. It publishes *The American Rifleman,* a monthly magazine which frequently has excellent articles of interest to gun collectors. Also, it publishes from time to time the names, meeting places, and dates of meeting of clubs for gun collectors all over the United States.

OHIO GUN COLLECTORS ASSOCIATION, Mrs. C. D. Rickey, Secretary, 130 Main Street, Prospect, Ohio. This club was organized in 1937 by Miller Bedford, New London, Ohio, who is active in its leadership. Most of the members live in Ohio, but any reputable United States citizen is eligible if properly recommended. It is generally regarded as the "grandfather" of most of the gun collectors' clubs in America and has conducted some of the most outstanding exhibitions of firearms in the United States.

SOUTHERN CALIFORNIA ARMS COLLECTORS ASSOCIATION, Richard B. Stanley, Secretary, 841 S. Donna Beth Avenue, West Covina, California, is probably the second oldest gun collectors' club in America. It conducts muzzle-loading matches and gun exhibitions and meets monthly in various cities in Los Angeles County.

CALIFORNIA MUZZLE-LOADERS AND COLLECTORS' ASSOCIATION, Lee Crum, Secretary, 7638 Pioneer Boulevard, Whittier, California, is comparatively new but one of the largest clubs in the United States.

AUTHOR'S NOTICE: This list of clubs and associations is by no means complete. There are at least fifty gun collector's clubs affiliated with the National Rifle Association of America, scattered all over the United States and several hundred independent clubs. For information about a club near you, refer to *The American Rifleman, The Gun Report, Guns Magazine,* or similar publications. Also every full-time antique arms dealer is glad to give you the name, meeting place, and date of meeting of gun collectors' clubs.

PERIODICALS

The American Rifleman, published monthly by the National Rifle Association of America, 1600 Rhode Island Avenue, N.W., Washington 6, D.C. It publishes highly accurate and interesting articles for collectors although shooting is the principal subject.

The Gun Report, published monthly by World-Wide Gun Report, Inc., P.O. Box 111, Aledo, Illinois, primarily for collectors, with articles in each issue of interest to both beginners and advanced collectors.

Guns Magazine, published monthly by Publishers' Development Corporation, 8150 North Central Park Boulevard, Skokie, Illinois. Many of its articles are on shooting, but it includes excellent articles on gun collecting and the historic background of antique arms.

Muzzle Blasts, published monthly by the National Muzzle-Loading Rifle Association, 12 E. Franklin St., Shelbyville, Indiana for collectors in general with emphasis on muzzle-loader shooting.

Author's Notice on Periodicals: There are many magazines and newspapers which from time to time publish articles of interest to collectors, but the above list is especially recommended. In addition, there is an annual publication, *The Gun Digest,* published by The Gun Digest Co., Chicago 6, Illinois, of general interest to all firearms enthusiasts, which always carries an excellent section for collectors.

A GLOSSARY OF
GUN TERMS

AMMUNITION. Material used in charging firearms, including powder, shot, primers, and cartridge cases.

AMUSETTE. An early breechloader, mounted like a cannon but fired like a musket, made of brass, firing a half-pound ball.

ARQUEBUS. Same as Harquebus, an early military musket.

AUTOMATIC. Guns operated by recoil or the pressure of the powder gas for loading and firing.

BANDS. Strips of metal which encircle and hold together the barrel and stock of a gun.

BARREL. The metal tube of a gun whose purpose is to concentrate the gas generated by the explosion of the powder on the base of the bullet, and to give the bullet velocity and direction.

BATTERY. In a flintlock, the steel or iron plate against which the flint strikes to produce sparks, sometimes erroneously called the "frizzen."

BELL. Or swell of the muzzle, so called because the muzzle flares out in the shape of a bell.

BLUING. The colored finish of the metal parts of guns in various shades of blue and also black, produced by various chemical processes.

BLUNDERBUSS. An early smoothbore gun with a round or oval barrel, and a bell-shaped muzzle; the barrel is usually of a large bore to hold a number of missiles for scatter-fire.

BOLT. That part of the breech-loading rifle which pushes the cartridge into position and locks the mechanism to prevent its opening on discharge.

BORE. The interior of the barrel; also used to indicate caliber.

BREECH. The rear of the barrel, the mechanism of a breechloader.

BREECH BLOCK. The part of the breech-loading mechanism which closes the breech and receives the backward pressure of the explosion.

BROWNING. The brown colored finish of metal parts of a gun. "Bluing" and browning" are also used as verbs to mean the act of coloring gun parts.

BUCK AND BALL. A cartridge with a round ball and three buckshot.

BUCKSHOT. Small lead bullet, or large shot, usually a sporting load.

BULLET SHELL. An explosive bullet with a bursting charge in a tube.

BULL'S-EYE. The center of the target, a shot which hits the center.

BUTT. The rear portion of the gunstock which is placed against the shoulder in firing.

BUTT PLATE. The metal plate on the butt.

CALIBER, CALIBRE. The diameter of the bore, usually expressed in decimal fractions of an inch and measured between the lands. Also, the diameter of a projectile. In continental Europe, caliber is expressed in millimeters. See also GAUGE.

CANNELURE. A groove around a bullet to hold the lubricant, receive metal stripped from the bullet in passing through the barrel, or to hold the cartridge case to the bullet.

CANNON. Ordnance or artillery, usually too big to be carried by hand.

CAP. (1) A container for fulminate or other explosive used to ignite the powder for percussion guns. (2) The cover for a gun part such as the grip or butt.

CARBINE. A short-barreled rifle for mounted men.

CARTRIDGE. The container for an explosive charge which may or may not include the bullet. The modern cartridge is placed in the gun, ready to fire, but some early cartridges were broken and the contents emptied into the chamber or barrel.

CARTRIDGE CASE. A metal container for the explosive charge.

CATCH. A part of the mechanism for holding another part in a desired position, as the bayonet catch, safety catch, locking catch, etc.

CENTER-FIRE CARTRIDGE. One in which the priming composition is in a cap in the center of the base of the case.

CHAMBER. The part of the breech which holds the charge.

CHASSEPOT RIFLE. The French Army rifle with the breech closed with a sliding bolt.

CHECKERING. Roughening of the wood on a gun for ornamentation or to give the hand a better grip on its surface.

CHEEK-PIECE. A portion of the stock of a long gun for supporting the face in the proper position for aiming.

CHOKE. A narrowing of the bore of a gun to prevent undue scattering of shot.

CLIP. A device for holding several cartridges together so that they may be loaded simultaneously in the gun.

COCK. (1) The movable portion of the firing mechanism corresponding to the hammer on modern guns. (2) To place the cock in position ready to fire.

CORNED POWDER. The early name for powder made in grains as contrasted with the original dustlike powder.

CYLINDER. The chambered breech part of a gun which revolves around an axis to expose the cartridges successively for firing.

DAG. An early name for a short pistol, especially a wheel lock.

DAMASCENE. To decorate iron or steel with a peculiar wavy marking.

DAMASCUS. Strips of iron and steel welded together and twisted to give a pattern of contrasting colors on the surface of a gun barrel.

DETONATOR. An early name for a gun fired by a percussion cap.

DOUBLE-ACTION. A revolver cocked and fired by pressing the trigger.

EJECTOR. A device which throws out the fired cartridge case, or a firearm equipped with this device.

EROSION. The gradual enlargement of the gun bore by the action of the gases from the powder explosion.

EXPRESS BULLET, EXPRESS RIFLE. Originally referred to a bullet or rifle with a long range and low trajectory; sometimes refers to the use of a light explosive bullet of large caliber.

FINE SIGHT. Aiming so that only the top edge of the front sight is seen through the rear sight.

FIRING-PIN. That part of the firing mechanism which strikes the cap or primer to explode the powder charge.

FLARE-PISTOL. A large pistol used to fire flares for illumination or signaling.

FLINTLOCK. A firearm which ignites the powder with the spark made by the contact of flint against steel or iron.

FORE-ARM, or FORE-END. That part of the wooden stock which is under the barrel and forward of the trigger guard.

FRIZZEN. See Battery.

FULL SIGHT. An aim in which all of the front sight is seen through the rear sight.

FULMINATE. An explosive substance or compound which ignites when struck, such as fulminate of mercury.

GAUGE, GAGE. The diameter of the bore of a gun expressed in the number of balls of that diameter which are required to make a pound; thus, a "12-gauge" gun is one with a diameter of such size that 12 balls of lead, each fitting the bore, weigh one pound. This is sometimes called "12-bore."

GRIP. The part of the gun held by the right hand in aiming.

GROOVES. The channels cut in the bore of a gun to give the bullet a rotary motion.

GUARD. A protective device. The hand guard is the wooden part protecting the hand from a hot barrel. The trigger guard protects the trigger.

GUN. Also spelled "gonne" and "gunne" in early English, a firearm of any kind in America, but in England restricted to shotguns.

HAIR TRIGGER. A trigger requiring only a light touch for firing.

HAMMER. The part of the mechanism which strikes the primer directly, or strikes the firing pin. This is the definition which applies to arms beginning with the percussion period.

HAND GUN. Originally applied to the hand cannon; now means any firearm that is easily carried, especially pistols and revolvers.

HARQUEBUS. See Arquebus.

HIGH-POWER. Military and sporting rifles using small-caliber bullets driven by a large charge of smokeless powder.

IGNITION. The setting on fire of the powder.

LANDS. The portions of the original inner surface of a rifled gun left when the grooves are cut.

LEVER ACTION. A repeating mechanism operated by a hinged rod.

LOCK. (1) The firing mechanism. (2) To set the safety to prevent firing.

LOCK PLATE. An iron plate fastened on the stock of a gun for mounting the firing mechanism.

LONG ARM. Or long gun, a term for long-barreled firearms such as rifles, carbines, and muskets as distinguished from the "short arms," pistols and revolvers.

MACHINE GUN. An automatic gun firing small-arms ammunition. In the American military sense it refers to weapons fired from a mount, such as a bipod or a tripod; but Europeans tend to include automatic rifles under this classification. Gun collectors seldom include machine guns in their exhibits.

MAGAZINE. That part of a repeating firearm which holds cartridges to be fed into the gun.

MATCH. A wick or cord prepared to burn at a uniform rate, originally by soaking it in a solution of saltpeter.

MATCHLOCK. A firearm using a lighted match to ignite the powder.

MILLIMETER, MILLIMETRE. One thousandth of a meter, or .03937 inch; a measure used in continental Europe to designate caliber.

MINIÉ-BALL. A conical bullet with a cavity in its base which expands from the force of the powder gas and thus fits the grooves of the rifling; named for its inventor, a French officer.

MIQUELET LOCK. A flint-and-steel firearm having a mainspring on the outside of the lockplate and a short battery made in one piece with the pan cover. It followed the snaphance and preceded the true flintlock.

MUSKET. Originally a smoothbore long arm, but later applied to military shoulder weapons in general.

MUSKETOON. A short musket with a large smooth bore.

MUZZLE. The mouth, or forward end of a gun.

NEEDLE-GUN. A German Army rifle, adopted in 1841; invented by Dreyse; a needle-like rod struck the fulminate to ignite the powder, which was inside a paper cartridge with the bullet.

NIPPLE or TEAT. The opening or tube of a percussion gun on which was placed the cap containing the fulminate or priming material. Also called "tit" and "cone."

OPEN SIGHT. A rear sight having a notch instead of a hole for lining up the front sight and target.

OVAL-BORE RIFLING. A bore that is oval-shaped, the oval being twisted to give the bullet a spinning motion; this was developed to take the place of lands and grooves. Most rifles with this feature were made by Lancaster of London, about 1850.

PAN. The receptacle for priming powder in flint-and-steel arms, such as matchlock, wheel-lock, snaphance, miquelet lock, and flintlock.

PAN COVER. The lid or plate for protecting the priming powder against spilling or wetting.

PATCH. A wrapping of paper, linen, leather, or cloth originally used to facilitate the loading of the bullet in a muzzle-loader. Today, it refers to a metal jacket for the bullet, or a small cleaning cloth.

PATCH BOX. A receptacle often built into the stock of muzzle-loading rifles for carrying patches, grease, and small tools.

PEPPER BOX. A percussion pistol with several barrels revolving around a central axis and fired by a single fixed hammer.

PERCUSSION CAP. A small metal cup holding fulminate placed on the tube or nipple of a percussion gun; when struck, the sparks entered the barrel through a hole and fired the charge. Also applied to other priming systems, such as the Maynard.

PINS. Pieces of iron or steel used to hold the barrel and stock together, and to hold other parts together.

PISTOL. A small firearm with a short barrel, aimed and fired from one hand.

PISTOL CARBINE. A pistol with a detachable shoulder stock, so that it can be fired from either the hand or the shoulder.

PRIMER. The loose powder, pill, pellet, or "cap" used to ignite the main powder charge. In modern cartridges, the primer is built into the base or rear of the cartridge case.

PRIMING PAN. Same as PAN.

PRIMING POWDER. The gunpowder in the pan used to set off the main charge.

PUMP GUN. A repeating rifle, especially one with a lever suggestive of a pump handle.

PYRITES. A mineral substance, usually iron disulphide, commonly called "fool's gold," used in wheel-lock and pyrites-lock guns to make sparks when struck by steel or iron.

PYRITES LOCK. A predecessor of the true flintlock, not recognized by many historians.

RAMROD. (1) A rod of wood, iron, or steel for pushing the bullet into the muzzle-loader; (2) today it means a cleaning rod.

RANGE. The distance to the target; the maximum distance a bullet will travel.

RECOIL. The backward motion of a gun when fired, commonly called "kick."

REPEATER. A gun that can be fired several times without reloading, usually applied to rifles and carbines.

REST. Any support to steady the gun during aiming and firing; originally, the guns were so heavy that forked sticks were used.

REVOLVER. (1) A firearm, usually a pistol, with a cylinder of several chambers arranged to revolve on an axis and discharge the shots in succession by the same lock. (2) A firearm with several barrels revolving about a common axis.

RIFLE. A shoulder firearm having spiral grooves cut in its bore to obtain greater accuracy from the spinning motion given to the bullet; it differs from a carbine in having greater length and weight. Early rifling was sometimes straight, instead of spiral, but these were powder accumulation grooves, not true rifling.

SEAR. Spelled "SCEAR" in England, a pivoted pawl or latch in the lock of small arms, operating between the trigger and the hammer or striker.

SELF-LOADING. Semiautomatic; the fired cartridge is extracted and ejected and a live cartridge is placed in position, ready to fire.

SERPENTINE. Originally the name of the S-shaped metal part of the matchlock which held the lighted match, but later applied to gunpowder, and sometimes used as a synonym for matchlock.

SET TRIGGER. A trigger used to set the hair trigger.

SHELL. The case for holding the charge for breech-loaders.

SHOT. (1) A projectile. (2) Small pellets. (3) The number of bullets that can be fired without reloading, as "a 5-shot gun."

SHOTGUN. A firearm intended for the use of a number of small pellets rather than a single bullet.

SIGHT. An aiming device on a gun, such as "telescopic sight," "open sight," etc.

SLIDE ACTION. The mechanism of a repeating rifle operated by the manual movement of a slide under and parallel to the barrel.

SLING. A strap attached to a gun to carry it or to steady it in aiming.

SMALL ARMS. A military term for portable arms such as rifles, carbines, shotguns, pistols, and revolvers.

SMOOTHBORE. A gun with an unrifled bore.

SNAPHANCE. An early flint-and-steel firearm having a separate battery and pan cover with a snapping cock.

SPANNER. A wrench or "key" for winding the spring on a wheel lock.

SPHERICAL BULLET. One that is a round ball.

STOCK. The wooden part of a firearm; that portion which fits against the shoulder in firing.

STOPPAGE. Failure to function, a "jam."

STRIKER. A hammer or firing pin.

STUD. A projection on a gun for holding another part, such as the "bayonet stud" or the "sight stud."

SWIVEL GUN. One fired from a swivel mount, on a boat, wall, or animal.

SWIVELS. A link or coupling device which permits either of the attached parts to rotate independently of the other, such as the sling swivels, the stacking swivel, or a swivel ramrod.

TANG. A projecting shank, prong, or tongue, forming part of one object for joining it to another. Thus, a trigger guard may have projections at both ends for screwing it to the stock of the gun; both of these are "tangs."

TEAT. See Nipple or Teat. The "Teat" or "Tit-Fire" cartridge is an obsolete center-fire cartridge with the priming in a protruding "nipple" or "teat," which was struck by the hammer to fire.

TOUCHHOLE. The vent, or flash hole, or tube between the priming and the powder in the barrel.

TRAJECTORY. The path of the bullet through the air.

TRIGGER. The lock device pulled by the finger to release the cock or hammer and fire the piece.

TRIGGER GUARD. A metal loop or rectangle protecting the trigger.

TRIGGER PLATE. The portion of the mechanism through which the trigger enters.

VENT. Same as touchhole; on modern arms it is a gas-escape hole.

WALL PIECE. A firearm of large size, bore, and weight, often of the arquebus type, mounted on a swivel for firing from the wall of a fortress; or, a similar gun provided with a recoil plate or hook to be placed against the wall to absorb part of the recoil from firing.

WHEEL LOCK. An early firearm, historically between the matchlock and the flintlock, in which the spark was made by a wheel revolving against a piece of iron pyrite. The wheel lock in use overlapped both the matchlock and early forms of the wheel lock.

WORM. A screw fastened to the end of a ramrod for pulling the charge out of a muzzle-loading gun. This was necessary when the owner wanted to remove the bullet, powder, and patch, either as a safety measure, or when the gun failed to fire.

AUTHOR'S NOTICE REGARDING GLOSSARY. This Glossary, like the other portions of this text, is presented for the beginner and the intermediate collector. The definitions are more fully explained and illustrated in other gun books by the author, such as *The Gun Collector's Handbook of Values; Gun Care and Repair—A Manual of Gunsmithing; The Boy's Book of Rifles; Guns of the Old West;* and *The Art of Shooting.*

BIBLIOGRAPHY

Albaugh, William A., III, and Simmons, Edward N., *Confederate Arms*. Harrisburg, Pa.: The Stackpole Co., 1957.

Baker, Ezekiel, *Remarks on Rifle Guns* (also titled *Baker's Remarks on the Rifle*). London: Joseph Mallett, 1835.

Bannerman, David B., *Military Goods Catalogue*. New York: Francis Bannerman Sons, 1955, *et seq.*

Bartholomew, Ed, *The Biographical Album of Western Gunfighters*. Houston: The Frontier Press, 1958.

Bosworth, N., *A Treatise on the Rifle, Musket, Pistol and Fowling Piece*. New York: J. S. Redfield, 1846.

Brown, F. R. (Bob), *Encyclopedia of Modern Firearms—Parts & Assembly*, Vol. 1. Montezuma, Iowa: F. R. (Bob) Brownell, 1959.

Burrard, Gerald, *The Modern Shotgun* (in two volumes). New York: Charles Scribner's Sons, 1931.

Chapel, Charles Edward, *The Boy's Book of Rifles*. New York: Coward-McCann, Inc., 1948.

———— *Field, Skeet, and Trap Shooting*. New York: Coward-McCann, Inc., 1949.

———— *Forensic Ballistics*. Chicago: Institute of Applied Science, 1933.

———— *Gun Care and Repair—A Manual of Gunsmithing*. New York: Coward-McCann, Inc., 1943.

———— *The Gun Collector's Handbook of Values,* revised edition. New York: Coward-McCann, Inc., 1960.

———— *Simplified Rifle Shooting*. New York: Coward-McCann, Inc., 1950.

———— *The Art of Shooting*. New York: A. S. Barnes & Co., Inc., 1960.

———— *Guns of the Old West*. New York: Coward-McCann, Inc., 1960.

———— *Simplified Pistol and Revolver Shooting*. New York: Coward-McCann, Inc., 1950.

Clephan, Robert Coltman, *An Outline of the History and Develop-*

ment of Hand Firearms, etc. London: The Walter Scott Publishing Co., 1906.

Cline, Walter M., *The Muzzle-Loading Rifle, Then and Now.* Huntington, W. Va.: Standard Printing and Publishing Co., 1942.

Connecticut Historical Society, *Samuel Colt's Own Record of Transactions with Captain Walker and Eli Whitney, Jr., in 1847.* Hartford, Conn.: The Connecticut Historical Society, 1949.

Damon, G. E., *Gun Fun with Safety.* Huntington, W. Va.: Standard Publications, Inc., 1947.

Deane, *Deane's Manual of the History and Science of Fire-Arms.* London: Longman, Brown, Green, Longman's & Roberts, 1858.

Dillin, John G. W., *The Kentucky Rifle.* Wilmington, Delaware: George N. Hyatt, 1959.

Dougall, James Dalziel, *Shooting: Its Appliances, Practice, and Purpose.* London: Sampson Low, Marston, Searle & Rivington, 1881.

Edwards, William B., *The Story of Colt's Revolver.* Harrisburg, Pa.: The Stackpole Co., 1957.

Freidel, Frank, *The Splendid Little War.* Boston, Little, Brown & Co., 1958.

Fuller, Claud E., *The Breech-Loader in the Service.* Topeka, Kansas: F. Theodore Dexter, 1933.

———— *The Rifled Musket.* Harrisburg, Pa.: The Stackpole Co., 1958.

———— *Springfield Muzzle-Loading Shoulder Arms.* New York: Francis Bannerman Sons, 1930.

———— *The Whitney Firearms.* Huntington, W. Va.: Standard Publications, Inc., 1946.

———— and Steuart, Richard D., *Firearms of the Confederacy.* Huntington, W. Va.: Standard Publications, Inc., 1944.

Gardner, Robert E., *American Arms and Arms Makers.* Columbus, Ohio: The F. J. Heer Printing Co., 1938.

George, J. N., *English Guns and Rifles.* Plantersville, S.C.: Small-Arms Technical Publishing Co., 1947.

———— *English Pistols and Revolvers.* Onslow County, N.C.: Small-Arms Technical Publishing Co., 1938.

Gluckman, Arcadi, *Catalogue of United States Martial Pistols.* Buffalo: Otto Ulbrich Co., 1939.

———— *United States Martial Pistols and Revolvers.* Buffalo: Otto Ulbrich Co., 1939.

Gluckman, Arcadi, *United States Muskets, Rifles and Carbines.* Buffalo: Otto Ulbrich Co., Inc., 1948.

—————— and Satterlee, L. D., *American Gun Makers.* Harrisburg, Pa.: The Stackpole Co., 1953.

Grant, James, *More Single-Shot Rifles.* New York: William Morrow & Co., 1959.

—————— *Single-Shot Rifles.* New York: William Morrow & Co., 1947.

Gunther, Jack Disbrow, and Gunther, Charles O., *The Identification of Firearms.* New York: John Wiley & Sons, Inc., 1935.

Hardee, W. J., *Rifle and Light Infantry Tactics* (two or more volumes). Philadelphia: Lippincott, Grambo & Co., 1855.

Hatch, Alden, *Remington Arms in American History.* New York: Rinehart & Co., Inc.

Hatcher, Julian S., *Hatcher's Notebook.* Harrisburg, Pa.: Military Service Publishing Co., 1847.

—————— *Textbook of Firearms Investigation, Identification and Evidence.* Marines, Onslow County, N.C.: Small-Arms Technical Publishing Co., 1935.

Haven, Charles T., and Belden, Frank A., *A History of the Colt Revolver.* New York: William Morrow & Co., 1940.

Held, Robert, *The Age of Firearms.* New York: Harper & Brothers, 1957.

Hicks, James E.

    AUTHOR'S NOTICE: The books by James E. Hicks were published by him at Mt. Vernon, N.Y., thus:

Notes on United States Ordnance, Vol. 1, *Small Arms,* 1940.

Notes on United States Ordnance, Vol. II, *Ordnance Correspondence,* 1940.

Notes on German Ordnance, 1937.

Notes on French Ordnance, 1937.

Notes on French Ordnance (translation of *Mémoires d'Artillerie*), 1939.

    U.S. Firearms (revision of Vol. 1, above), 1946.

Hunter, J. Marvin, and Rose, Noah H., *The Album of Gun-Fighters.* San Antonio, Texas: Published by the Authors.

Johnson, Melvin M., Jr., and Haven, Charles T., *Automatic Weapons of the World.* New York: William Morrow & Co., 1945.

Kalman, James M., and Patterson, C. Meade, *Pictorial History of U.S. Single-Shot Martial Pistols*. New York: Charles Scribner's Sons, 1957.

Karr, Charles Lee, Jr., and Robbins, Carroll, *Remington Handguns*. Harrisburg, Pa.: The Stackpole Co., 1951.

Leffingwell, William Bruce, *The Art of Wing Shooting*. Chicago: Rand, McNally & Co., 1894.

Lenz, Ellis Christian, *Muzzle Flashes*. Huntington, W. Va.: Standard Publications, Inc., 1944.

———— *Rifleman's Progress*. Huntington, W. Va.: Standard Publications, Inc., 1946.

Logan, Herschel C., *Cartridges—A Pictorial Digest of Small Arms Ammunition*. Huntington, W. Va.: Standard Publications, Inc., 1948.

———— *Hand Cannon to Automatic*. Huntington, W. Va.: Standard Publications, Inc., 1944.

McClellan, George B., *Manual of Bayonet Exercises, Prepared for the Use of the United States Army*. Philadelphia: J. B. Lippincott & Co., 1852.

McConnell, Duncan, *Grandpappy's Pistol*. New York: Coward-McCann, Inc., 1956.

McGivern, Ed, *Ed McGivern's Book on Fast and Fancy Revolver Shooting and Police Training*. Springfield, Mass.: King Richardson Co., 1938.

McHenry, Roy C., and Roper, Walter F., *Smith & Wesson Hand Guns*. Harrisburg, Pa.: The Stackpole Co., 1958.

Mayer, Dr. Joseph R., *Five Centuries of Gunsmiths, Swordsmiths and Armourers, 1400–1900*. Columbus, Ohio: Walter F. Heer, 1948.

Metschl, John, *The Rudolph J. Nunnemacher Collection of Projectile Arms*. Milwaukee: The Milwaukee Public Museum, 1928.

Nutter, Waldo E., *Manhattan Firearms*. Harrisburg, Pa.: The Stackpole Co., 1958.

Parsons, John E., *Henry Deringer's Pocket Pistol*. New York: William Morrow & Co., 1952.

———— *The Peacemaker and Its Rivals*. New York: William Morrow & Co., 1950.

———— *Smith & Wesson Revolvers: The Pioneer Single-Action Models*. New York: William Morrow & Co., 1957.

Parsons, John E., and duMont, John S., *Firearms in the Custer Battle*. Harrisburg, Pa.: The Stackpole Co., 1954.

Pollard, H. B. C., *A History of Firearms*. London: Geoffrey Bles, 1931; Boston: Houghton Mifflin Co., 1931.

Rohan, Jack, *Yankee Arms Maker*. New York: Harper & Brothers, 1948.

Rosebush, Waldo E., *Frontier Steel, The Men and Their Weapons*. Appleton, Wis.: C. C. Nelson Publishing Co., 1958.

Russell, Carl P., *Guns of the Early Frontiers*. Berkeley, Calif.: University of California Press, 1957.

Rywell, Martin, *Samuel Colt, A Man and an Epoch*. Harriman, Tenn.: Pioneer Press, 1952.

Sandoz, Mari, *The Buffalo Hunters*. New York: Hasting House Publishers, 1954.

Satterlee, L. D., *A Catalog of Firearms for the Collector*. Detroit: Published by the author, 1939.

Sawyer, Charles Winthrop.
    AUTHOR'S NOTICE: All of these were originally published by Charles Winthrop Sawyer.
    Firearms in American History, 1600–1800.
    Firearms in American History, Vol. II, *The Revolver, 1800–1911*. (An authorized reprint edition of 1,000 copies was published in 1939 by Charles Edward Chapel.)
    Firearms in American History, Vol. III, *Our Rifles*.
    United States Single-Shot Martial Pistols.

Scott, Winfield, *Abstract of Infantry Tactics*. Boston: Hilliard, Gray, Little & Wilkins, 1830.

———— *Infantry Tactics in Three Volumes*. New York: Harper & Brothers, 1858.

Serven, James E., *Colt Firearms*. Santa Ana, Calif.: James E. Serven, 1954.

Sharpe, Philip B., *The Rifle in America*. New York: Funk & Wagnalls Co., 1938.

Sherlock, Herbert Arment, *Black Powder Snapshots*. Huntington, W. Va.: Standard Publications, Inc., 1946.

Shields, Joseph W., *From Flintlock to M-1*. New York: Coward-McCann, Inc., 1954.

Smith, Lawrence B., *Shotgun Psychology*. New York: Charles Scribner's Sons, 1938.

Smith & Wessen, Inc., *Burning Powder*. Springfield, Mass.: Smith & Wesson, Inc., 1921, *et seq.*

Stevens, Captain C. A., *Berdan's United States Sharpshooters in the Army of the Potomac, 1861–65*. St. Paul, Minn.: Price-McGill Co., 1892.

Ulrich, Arthur L., *A Century of Achievement, 1836–1936, Colt's 100th Anniversary Fire Arms Manual*. Hartford, Conn.: Colt's Patent Fire Arms Manufacturing Co., 1936.

Van Rensselaer, Stephen, *An Histology of American Gunsmiths, Arms Manufacturers, and Patentees with Detailed Description of Their Arms*. Morristown, N. J.: Mrs. Stephen Van Rensselaer, 1947.

Williamson, Harold F., *Winchester, The Gun that Won the West*. Washington, D.C.: Combat Force Press, 1952.

Winant, Lewis, *Early Percussion Firearms*. New York: William Morrow & Co., 1959.

———— *Firarms Curiosa*. New York: Greenberg, Publisher, 1955.

———— *Pepperbox Firearms*. New York: Greenberg, Publisher, 1952.

INDEX